THE PROMISE

THE PROMISE

How One Woman Made

Good on Her Extraordinary Pact

to Send a Classroom of First

Graders to College

ORAL LEE BROWN

with Caille Millner

DOUBLEDAY

New York   London   Toronto   Sydney   Auckland

PUBLISHED BY DOUBLEDAY
a division of Random House, Inc.

DOUBLEDAY and the portrayal of an anchor with a dolphin
are registered trademarks of Random House, Inc.

Book design by rlf design

Cataloging-in-Publication Data is on file with the Library of Congress.
ISBN 0-385-51147-7

PRINTED IN THE UNITED STATES OF AMERICA
May 2005

First Edition

1 3 5 7 9 10 8 6 4 2

This is dedicated to the twenty-three students
from Brookfield Elementary School. Seventeen years ago
I walked into their lives and I have not let go. We have become a
family that has withstood the test of time. We have shared the
good times and forgotten about the bad times. We have celebrated
birthdays and graduations and we have mourned
at funerals. But through it all we made it.

Contents

Prologue: The Angel

One night in December 1987, I hid in my car while the media hunted all over Oakland, California, for me. I was scared to death, and not because I had tried to do something wrong. All I had tried to do was something impossible, or at least that's what most people would say. I walked into a classroom in one of East Oakland's toughest neighborhoods, took a look at twenty-three first-graders who nobody thought would amount to anything, and made them all a promise. "If you stay in school and graduate, I will pay to send you to college," I told them. Now, I didn't make this promise to get attention. When I walked into that classroom, I hadn't planned to promise anyone anything. And when I got home, I didn't even tell my husband or my own children what I had done. But somehow the news got out, and now everybody in the Bay Area wanted to know how in the world Oral Lee Brown—a woman who grew up poor in Mississippi, a woman who still wasn't making more than $45,000 a year—how in the world was Oral Lee Brown going to send twenty-three kids to college.

Well, you know what? The first time I walked into Brookfield Elementary I certainly didn't have the answer. My original goal wasn't to adopt anybody. Instead I was looking for one little girl who should have been going to school there, and the only reason I was looking for her was because I couldn't sleep at night. This little girl would have lived near Brookfield, which is in one of the worst neighborhoods in Oakland. In 1987 that was really saying something. That was the time of the crack wars and the place was full of dope, crime, and killing. Thirty percent of the city's children were living in poverty. The crime rate was one of the highest in the state and the country. Every parent I spoke to said that she felt trapped in her own neighborhood, even though there weren't any walls or gates. Trapped in the mind, is what she meant. And trapped by circumstances. There were no jobs, no legit jobs anyway, and to most people it didn't seem like there was a way to get out. It had gotten so bad that most parents had given up on their dreams for their kids. "I did my best," they'd all say, and turn their heads when they found out their kids were selling or using drugs. If she's in her right mind, a mother is going to overlook anything to feed her kids.

I understand where that attitude comes from because I've been hungry myself. But I wasn't expecting to find it in a little child. You see, about six weeks before I adopted that class at Brookfield Elementary, I was walking to the Hub Liquor Store on 94th Avenue. It was in the fall, late October, and at a time of morning when every kid should have been in school. I worked in the area, still do, and every morning I used to stop by that store to pick up a pack of Spanish peanuts and a Pepsi. Suddenly a little girl ran up to me and asked, "Lady, can I have a quarter?"

She looked like any six- or seven-year-old kid. If she had not asked me for the quarter, I never would have known she needed something to eat. As it was I guessed that she just wanted some candy or a soda or something that her mama couldn't afford to get her, but I figured that a child should have that, so I told her, "Come with me into the store." She followed me without a word, which was when I started to worry. What if I had been a rapist or a kidnapper? She would have walked off with me and not even blinked.

We walked into the store, and I put my peanuts and Pepsi on the counter while this little girl wandered up and down the aisles. It's not a big store, so it didn't take long before she showed up at the counter with bread, bologna, and cheese. Not a soda. Not candy. She wanted me to buy her some real food—the type of food that ought to have been in her mother's kitchen already. She put it all on the counter and looked up at me, like she was expecting me to say no. I didn't even know what to say. I just stood there holding my five-dollar bill, which was all the money I had. Al, who owns Hub Liquors and who knows me well, rang everything up. It came to $5.86, but he didn't say anything. He just put my soda and peanuts in one bag and the little girl's groceries in another, and that was it.

Or that should have been it. But I was flabbergasted. I looked at this child and I said, "Where is your mother?" In my mind, what I was really asking her was this: Why isn't your mother out trying to get some food? Because it was evident from the items that she purchased that this girl was hungry. Her whole family was probably hungry too. Maybe she had little brothers and sisters she was looking after—I didn't know. All I knew was that as far as I was concerned, this kid needed to be in school getting an education, not in the streets trying to seek resources for her household. And if she had to spend her days asking people for enough quarters to bring home bread and bologna, then when did she have time to go to school?

The little girl picked up her bag of food and skipped ahead of me. "Hey!" I shouted after her. "Did you hear me?" She stopped in the doorway of Hub Liquors as I repeated my question. "Where is your mother?" I asked again. "At home," said the girl, and she ran off. I walked out of the store and watched her go. She bounced down 94th Avenue and made a right turn on A Street. That was the last time I saw her.

And I guess most people would have let her go after that. I had done my good deed. I had bought her food—with my last five dollars, no less. That's more than enough as far as most people are concerned. After all, how many times a day does someone ask you for change, or hold up a sign asking you to buy them something? I'd lose track if I tried to count how often that happens to me, and like most people, I usually just keep on stepping. But this little girl wouldn't leave me alone. I couldn't get her out of my head. Every morning I went to Hub Liquors around the same time, hanging around just a little bit longer than usual in the hope that I might see her. I asked Al if he had ever seen her before or since, and he hadn't. "Keep my eyes open for you, though," he said, and I thanked him. But he never saw her again, either.

It started disturbing my sleep. Every night when I closed my eyes, this little girl's face floated behind them. I don't know what I felt—I wasn't concerned that she was in trouble or needed help, but something about the image of her little face troubled me. It got so bad after about two weeks that I called my older brother, EQ. Now EQ is somebody who I have faith in, somebody I respect. I don't call him unless I really feel like there's a problem I can't get hold of by myself. So I called him and told him what had happened. He listened patiently. He said, "Oral, I know this is troubling you, and the fact is it's a troubling situation. But you gave all you had that day. What more can you do?"

I said, "I don't know, EQ, but we need to do something. When I close my eyes I see this little girl."

He said, "Oral, you bought her food. You didn't even have enough money left for yourself that day. What else do you think you could do? You don't even know this girl's name."

"I don't know," I said, "but I need to do something. This child won't let me go to bed at night."

The only thing I could think of was that I needed to find this little girl. I didn't have any particular plan in mind other than to talk to her and find out why she was haunting me. I really don't know what I would have asked her. Maybe, Where have you been? Why did you disappear? Why are you out on the streets like that? Don't you know what can happen to little girls who talk to strangers? To tell you the truth, probably none of those questions would have gotten the answer I needed to get from her, which was a simple one: Why isn't somebody looking after you?

That's the question I ask every time I meet a kid who nobody wants to be accountable for—and it's usually a poor kid, and way too often it's a black kid or a Latino one. I ask the parents, I ask the community. I've been asking for years. And so far, I've never gotten a good enough answer. Probably because there *isn't* a good enough answer about why nobody seems to care about these kids.

And I don't just mean the kids out on the street. I mean all the kids who aren't graduating from high school, the dropouts, the ones who people say can't achieve—well, why not? And whose fault is that? It's not the child's fault. He came into this life with two eyes, two ears, a mouth, and everything else that qualifies him to be educated. I'm a firm believer that kids fail because we don't teach them how to succeed. It's as simple as that. If you walked into a first-grade classroom at Brookfield Elementary and asked the students how many of them wanted to be dummies when they grew up, they would laugh you right out of there. Nobody, and I mean nobody, wants to be a dummy.

But I didn't know all that then. I just wanted to see this little girl again. I wanted to try to figure out why she was haunting my sleep. She wasn't coming back to Hub Liquors, and I knew I wouldn't get anywhere looking for her there. I had doubts about whether or not she went to school frequently—she probably had to beg pretty often if she was looking to buy bologna and bread at her age—but I know it's illegal to keep your kids from school all the time, and I figured she had to be going to *some* school sometime, *somewhere*. So the day after I talked to EQ I looked in the phone book to find out what elementary school she would have been attending. After I made a couple of calls I found out that the local school was Brookfield, and that the principal was a lady named Mrs. Yolanda Peeks.

I called the secretary and scheduled an appointment with

Mrs. Peeks. I wanted to explain the situation to her in person, so she could see that I was hardworking and clean-living, not some weirdo. And to her credit, I don't think Mrs. Peeks ever doubted me. She invited me into her office and listened while I talked. I told her basically what had happened: that I had met the girl outside of Hub Liquors, that she needed food that day—and real food, not snacks—and that I went back to the same place every morning to look for her. I told her that I was disturbed by the fact that this little girl was out trying to get food for her home when she needed to be in school.

I told her that I was especially disturbed because what if, instead of meeting me that morning, the girl had encountered a criminal? She had followed me into the store, she would have followed him anywhere. The rapist could have said, "Come on baby, I'll get you a quarter, but it's in my car." And I think she would have followed him right to his car, or to a dark corner of a park, or wherever. All she was thinking about was that this is a person who is going to give me a quarter so that I can eat. And I don't know what Mrs. Peeks thought of all this, but at this point she advised me that they had two first-grade classes and I could look for her in both of them. She even escorted me to those classrooms personally.

So we went to the two first-grade classes. I saw lots of other bright, energetic kids, all ready to learn and totally uninformed about how little people expected from them—but I didn't see the little girl I was looking for. After we left the second classroom, I must have looked pretty downhearted, because Mrs. Peeks glanced at me and said, "I think there are some children absent today. Let's go back to my office and find out who's not here. Maybe your little girl is one of the ones who isn't here today."

Remember that I didn't know the child's name—and for that matter, I still don't. But the point is that I didn't have a clue whether or not any of the children who were absent would have been her. The only way for me to know would be if I saw the child in front of me. But we went back to Mrs. Peeks's office, and Mrs. Peeks asked her secretary to pull up the attendance rolls. We studied them and found out that there were three girls missing from the first grade that day.

So Mrs. Peeks asked me what I wanted to do, and the only thing I could think of was that I wanted to come back and see the girls who were missing. I asked her if she would call me on a day when all the first-graders were present. She agreed to do so, and I went back home.

A few days later I got a call from Mrs. Peeks's office informing me that all the first-graders were in class, and if I still wanted to do so, I should come down and see if any of the children were the little girl I was looking for. I drove over to Brookfield, and Mrs. Peeks was kind enough to escort me to the classrooms again.

Now, supposedly all the first-graders were there that day. When we went into each classroom, the teachers gathered all of their students together in a clump, like a bunch of flowers, at the front of the room so that I could look at them. All those happy little faces! At this point I didn't look at them too closely, because I was just looking for this one little girl. Right then, I just saw lots of shiny little smiles—but none of them belonging to the little girl I was looking for.

I don't know that you can imagine how I felt about this—I

don't know how to explain, except to say that I felt almost ready to give up. All that stress and effort and she still wasn't there. Not to mention what I'd put Mrs. Peeks and the teachers and all these other kids through. I had disrupted Mrs. Pecks's day twice, calling her out of the blue and then having her traipse through these classrooms with me. I had broken into the teachers' lessons, asking them to get all their students together so I could look at them. And of course, the poor kids, I had them stand in front of me like I was a magician at a fair, and then I had rejected them all. They didn't even know why I was there or what was going on. All they knew was that some strange lady hadn't found them to be what she wanted. Which I guess was something they'd already been through too many times in their lives.

So that's how I was feeling at that moment, and to be honest, I don't know what happened to me. As I said, I wasn't planning to adopt anybody. I was just looking for one little girl who had moved me—and really, any child who was hungry like that would have moved me, so I'm not even sure why it was that particular child. But she was the one I ran into on that morning in front of the liquor store, and she was the one I was looking for, for the simple reason that I needed some peace.

But now I wasn't going to get that peace, and I had to say something to this teacher and the twenty-three little faces in front of me. I turned away from the students, and without thinking I said to Mrs. Peeks, "Mrs. Peeks, is it all right if I adopt the class?"

Well, she could have fallen over. I have to give credit to Mrs. Peeks, because she hadn't thought I was out of my mind up until this point. She knew I was serious when I walked in her door, and she gave me the benefit of the type of doubt that quite a few people would not have been able to do. Later on, of course, she was one of the people who I depended on to make everything happen, and she's still very important to the work I do. She's never been anything but a rock, but at the moment I asked her if I could adopt the class she must have had a few questions about me! I can remember her saying, "Lady, who are you?" And then she answered that question for herself: "Lady, I don't know *who* you are, but you are crazy!"

Was I crazy?

Some people would say so. There sure were enough of them who told me so over the years. But I'm glad that I didn't think too much about it just then, and I'm really glad that Mrs. Peeks pulled herself together to help me. She just picked her jaw up off the ground and started asking practical questions, like exactly what I wanted to do when I said I wanted to adopt the class. We walked into the hallway to discuss it, and at this point we didn't get too specific. I was speaking off the top of my head, because I hadn't given it any thought. At the time I only made about $45,000 a year!

First of all, I told Mrs. Peeks that I would give $10,000 a year to a trust fund for these kids' college educations. We could set up a foundation to make sure the money was being invested properly, is what I think I said. The one thing I *did* know from the beginning was that this project was going to be about getting these kids into college—to my mind every kid should have the chance to go to college. It's my belief that if you start young enough with any child and instill in them the importance of education, maybe, just maybe, by the time that child gets to twelfth grade he or she will be ready for college. And I felt that with me and the teachers and the principals behind them that these kids had a real shot at finishing high school. That may not sound like much, but Castlemont High School, which is where most of the students would go, had a 20 percent dropout rate. What happens to those kids? Is nobody accountable for them? Does nobody care about them?

That wasn't going to happen to my kids. I told Mrs. Peeks that I would need access to the classroom, so that I could work with the students and help their teachers out. They could search my background to make sure I wasn't a criminal; I had no problem with that. If I was going to adopt them, I told Mrs. Peeks, I needed to be a real presence in their lives.

Of course I didn't anticipate what "being a real presence" would turn out to mean. I just thought it meant going to the school and saving the money. Simple. In my mind at that moment — and remember I was making this up as I went along — I was going to spend some time at the school, help the kids' teachers out, and then I would go back home and go to my office.

It didn't work that way at all.

I became a parent to twenty-three students. As soon as they got big enough to start dialing my phone number, I was the outlet. I was the person they could say anything to. That's because my role was to love them, not to discipline them. I was the person who, no matter what, they could come to with their troubles. If they got upset with mommy, they could tell me. If they got upset with their teachers, they could tell me. If they had a problem that they didn't feel they could share with any other adult, I became their sounding board. Twenty-three kids. That's a lot more than going to the school every once in a while and saving the money! But that's what you have to accept when you decide to really play a role in your community, your time is no longer your own, but there will be rewards that you may not have expected when you made that decision to give up your time.

Back in the first-grade classroom, Mrs. Peeks was listening to me and shaking her head. She couldn't believe it. "Is that what you want to do?" she asked. And I nodded like I knew what I was talking about, and she said, kind of stunned, that it was fine. "I'll have to get approval from the Board of Education," she said. "They'll have to run some checks on you."

"That's fine with me," I said. "Just give me a call when everything's done and you're ready for me to come in and start helping the kids." She sure must have thought I had lost my mind!

So I went home. And, you know, I didn't even tell my husband or my own children—I have two daughters who were grown by then—what I had done. I don't know why, except that I didn't consider this something that I needed to share with other people. It was something I did for myself and that little girl; something I needed to do so that I could sleep at night. That is exactly how I considered it. Because it's interesting, as soon as I adopted the class, I could sleep at night, even though I never met that little girl again. I sure tried to find her. I looked for her for *years*. For a long while I was even suspicious of Mrs. Peeks, thinking that maybe someone *had* been absent from school when I'd visited. That maybe she was absent so often no one bothered to expect her in school, but that one day I would walk into a classroom and see her.

When the days turned into months and the months turned into years, it became clear to me that I was not going to see that little girl at Brookfield, but I still wondered about her. What did she look like now? Where was she? Why couldn't we find her? I would have had all kinds of questions for this girl if I were to see her again, which is funny because surely she wouldn't remember me. She was just six or seven years old, how would she remember some woman who bought her food one morning? But I, and pretty much everyone else who became involved in what was to become the Oral Lee Brown Foundation, looked and looked for her. Even now, she crosses my mind every time I'm walking around 94th Avenue. She would be twenty-two, twenty-three, maybe even twenty-four now, and maybe if she walked up to me I wouldn't even know who she was. But as soon as I figured it out I would have some questions for her. Where have you been? What have you done for the last seventeen years? Did you finish school? Why couldn't we find you? Did you ever think about me?

I know this sounds funny. I also know that I'll never see this child again. But I still wonder about her, because the fact is that she was the impetus behind this whole enterprise. That's why she's so important to me. Up until about three years ago, I was still looking for her and trying to figure out what had happened to her. She was still in the back of my mind, her face, her presence . . . even though I hadn't had trouble sleeping for a long time. She didn't *bother* me like she once had. But she was *there*, in a way that made me wonder if I could still find her if I just looked hard enough.

Then, the year my first-graders graduated from high school, I got a very interesting phone call. The lady on the line had seen me on television, talking about my kids who were graduating and the little girl who started all of this. "I remember when you adopted that class of kids," the lady told me. "I read about it in the newspaper, and I said to my husband, There is no way that woman can get those kids through school."

Well, everybody else said that too, so I wasn't too impressed by *that* comment, but I was sure surprised at what came next. "I'd like to give your foundation $10,000," she said. "Don't use my name or anything—I'd like it to stay anonymous. But I do have one request for you."

"What's that?" I asked. I was still picking myself up off the floor after she said $10,000!

"Stop worrying about that little girl," she said. "You know, the one you met at the liquor store all those years ago? Stop looking for her."

"And why's that?" I asked, and I hope I didn't say it too mean. I didn't want to offend someone who had just offered to give the foundation $10,000, but on the other hand, why was she telling me to stop looking for that child? She wasn't there that morning. She didn't know what I had been living through because of my memory of that little girl.

"That child's not coming back," said the lady. "In fact, she was supposed to disappear. She was an angel, and she came to you because you were meant to get involved with those kids."

Now, I didn't say what I was thinking. I've learned how to hold my tongue around people who've just given us a lot of money, and I was really impressed by this lady. A whole lot of people who give money do it because they want their name in the paper, or they want people to stop them on the street and congratulate them. Basically they want to give for themselves, as much as for the kids. But this lady wanted to stay anonymous. I give a lot of weight to that, because she was just interested in seeing the kids do well, not in getting some kind of attention for herself. But that doesn't mean I took her advice well at all. *At all.* What I was thinking was, Well, thank you, but I don't think angels need to eat and I know what this girl bought at the store.

And that might have been the end of it, except a couple of days later I was on the phone with my good friend Joanne Baker. I've known Joanne for years—Joanne works at a title company and I work in real estate, and she was the president of the foundation's board for about ten years. She's stood by me through all of this, and from the very beginning, which is something that I can't say about a lot of people. So let's just say that I know her very well, and she knows a whole lot about me. What she didn't know that particular day was that I had gotten a call from a lady who told me that the little girl we had spent so much time and energy looking for was an angel. And I wasn't about to tell her because I was still feeling so strange about the phone call myself.

So you can guess how strange I felt when Joanne told me the exact same thing. "Joey, you need to get off the phone," I snapped, as soon as Joanne said the word "angel." I was truly afraid. I hadn't said anything to Joanne about this lady's phone call, but here she was telling me the exact same thing just a couple of days later. Now, I'm not hardheaded. If someone tells me something I step back and listen, even if I don't agree. I had never heard Joanne talk about angels before, so in my mind, this meant that she must know something that I didn't know—something must have told her that I needed to stop looking for the little girl because I would never find her.

I really don't know where she might have gotten that message from, but I sure knew that Someone was trying to tell *me* something. I got the message the second time loud and clear. Sure, I can argue back and forth that she wasn't an angel until I'm blue in the face. *Yeah, Oral,* I say to myself, *if you had bought the food and looked around and she had disappeared then you could have said, Yeah, maybe I imagined that little girl. But Al actually gave her the bag, so there was a witness that she was there . . .* But that's really not the point anymore. I got the message and I'm at peace now. I've chalked it up to God.

But you see, that peace took a long time for me to find. A *long* time. And in that long time, I had to raise and educate twenty-three kids. Which brings me back to that night in December 1987, that night when I was hiding in my car from the media and Lord knows what else. Probably what I was really hiding from were my own worries about this whole thing. I was just starting to worry at that point. Because you know, when I walked out of that first-grade classroom after making my promise to those children, I wasn't worried. I didn't even think about it. It was only then, a couple of weeks later, that I started to get afraid. *What* had I done? And most important, *how* was I going to do this? How was I going to get these kids through twelve years of school, then pay for their college education when everybody said it was impossible?

I was about to find out.

I

The Education of Oral Lee Brown

Even though I acted as a surrogate parent to twenty-three kids, I didn't always understand what they were going through growing up. I couldn't compare my childhood to theirs at all. Even though I'm just in my early sixties, and was only in my forties when I made my promise, the world of my childhood has disappeared. Well, in most ways, I hope!

I was born in Mississippi in the early 1940s, in a small town just outside Batesville. At the time Batesville, which is on the Tallahatchie River about fifty miles southwest of Memphis, Tennessee, had a population of about 15,000 people. The most interesting thing about Batesville when I was growing up was the fact that it was on the main train line that wound through the country, so we got to see all kinds of people coming and going when we were children. We also got to dream of leaving on that train, and believe you me, did I dream of leaving Mississippi! Even as a child I knew that there had to be a better life for me somewhere else, somewhere with racial integration and economic opportunity.

I am the ninth of twelve children born to Walter and Nezzie Bivins. My parents are old-fashioned farming folk: we grew cotton and corn, and we were very proud of the fact that we were one of the only black families in Batesville who owned our own land. Almost every other black family worked as sharecroppers, which meant that they did all the hard work on another man's land and then had to give most of the profit right back to the owner. That's why black people in the South stayed poor.

My father worked as a sharecropper for years and years before he saved up enough money to buy that land, and then we cleared and tilled it ourselves. When I say "we," I mean *all* of us—even at the age of eight years old I was picking fifty pounds of cotton a day, and then going back in the house to cook for twelve people. This was the time in my life when I learned a lot of the discipline—not to mention the penny-pinching—that it took to put an entire class of children through college.

You see, when you're picking cotton, you're doing it with the understanding that there's not a lot of money to be made in it. In fact, you're breaking your back for almost nothing. I'll give you an example: my family was so disciplined about working our own sixty acres that some years, we finished our crop in time to work on another farm that hadn't finished all the picking. We were paid every day for the amount of cotton that we picked, and so I can tell you exactly how much the fifty pounds of cotton that I picked every day at the age of eight years old was worth: two dollars. I remembered that later on when I was struggling to save enough money to put my babies through college: *Oral Lee*, I said to myself, *you used to work for two dollars a day. You can get through this.* And I always did.

It was a hard life in Mississippi. It was hard not just economically but socially, too. Thanks to segregation, black people had to live in a part of town called the Vance Bottom, down by the river, while white people lived up the hill in Batesville proper. Every few years the river flooded and destroyed many homes, and do you think any of those white people ventured down the hill to help out? That's right—they didn't. But they still expected black people to move off of the sidewalk when a white person passed by, and to keep their mouths shut after a black person was lynched by a white mob. That happened fairly often, too. Mississippi was a violent place to be a child.

In many ways, I'm one of the lucky ones. I left home when I was twelve years old. What happened was that one of my older sisters, Willie Bea, married a young man named Paul and followed him to Newburgh, New York. They had heard there were good jobs up North, and they wanted to escape segregation. They also started having children nearly every year of their marriage, including two sets of twins! They eventually had eight children in all. That would have been far too many babies for Willie Bea to manage by herself, so I lobbied my mother to be the one who got to leave Mississippi and help out.

After Mississippi, New York was amazing. When I arrived there at the age of twelve, everything about it felt completely foreign and new. It was the first time I had ever seen snow. It was the first time I'd ever seen a city! It was also the first time I had attended desegregated schools, and the first time I'd seen black people on an equal footing with white people. Of course there was still subtle segregation, but for the most part, everyone was just trying to make money in New York. I felt my heart bursting with pride when I saw black people who had "made it"—black people who had nice homes and nice cars just like the rich white people.

Now, when I say that I was one of the lucky ones, I mean I was lucky because I got out of Mississippi. In a different way, though, I wasn't lucky at all: I had to leave my mother, who I loved more than life itself. There's no way to describe how much I missed her during those years in New York, and how much I continued to miss her when I was an adult. In fact, after I was an adult, I used to tell my mother in the same breath that while I was so happy she had let me go to New York—where I didn't have to live under segregation—I also felt that she shouldn't have sent me away. I believe both of those things with all of my heart, even though they contradict each other. And my mother used to laugh at my logic whenever I said that, but she understood.

"Oral Lee," she told me, "there's no way I could've pleased you. What would you have liked me to do?"

"I'd have liked you to have packed up and gotten on that train with me," I told her. "All of us should have moved to New York."

She just laughed and laughed. The truth is that my mother probably wouldn't have liked New York. She's a Southerner in every way. Much later on, when all of her children were living in California, she moved to California too. Even though we all loved it, she never really got used to living there. As hard as her life was there, Mississippi was her home. I appreciate that—but I still wish that I could've put her in my suitcase when I moved to New York.

Even though I only lived in Mississippi for twelve years, I had two crucial experiences there that shaped my life. The first thing that happened was that I met a young woman who taught me the importance of education.

I've noticed that a lot of people who have gone on to do work in education had a special teacher during their childhood. If you read the autobiographies of educators like Helen Keller or Booker T. Washington, you'll notice that, even though they started their lives with huge disadvantages, there was someone in their childhood who mentored them and encouraged them; someone who believed in them. For me, that person was Miss Grace.

Miss Grace was not from Batesville. I believe she was from a big town in the South, maybe Memphis. She lived in the town of Batesville, in a house that was set up especially for young female teachers from out of town. There were a few teachers who came from hotshot cities to teach us ragged kids in Batesville; I'm sure there were white women who did this for the white schools too. A number of young teachers lived in Miss Grace's house, staying in their own apartments and boarding together. Young women didn't stay on their own then like they do now. And Miss Grace was young — she must have been about twenty-two years old, fresh out of college.

She was also beautiful. I'm not just saying that because she was the kindest lady you'd ever meet in your life! She was truly a pretty woman, and all the men in town used to stare at her. But she was one of those people who didn't even notice that kind of attention, because even though she was pretty she wasn't a snob. She was just everything that you could ever want to be: kind, beautiful, charming, gracious, sweet, intelligent, concerned. My brother Homer also had her as a teacher and even after we were grown we used to talk about how much we loved her. She was the sort of person who everyone loved.

Now, I always said she liked me because I was the ugliest kid in the class. The other kids used to say, "Why does Miss Grace like that ugly girl?" But it didn't bother me. First of all, I was just happy to be in school in the first place. See, unlike the way things are for kids today, when I was growing up kids were either in school or they were working in the fields. So we were *all* thrilled to be in that schoolhouse. There was never any question of "cutting class" like kids do today. If a kid was absent from school, it was because his parents needed him to be at work in the fields. That happened to all of us around harvesting time, and we were always sorry to leave our lessons.

I was doubly sorry to leave Miss Grace. For the first time, in addition to having someone at home who loved me—that's my mother, I was always special to my mother—I now had someone out in the world who loved me too. I often thought about how I came to play Miss Grace's role in the lives of my students. And when I got frustrated or upset with my students, I thought of Miss Grace, and that gave me peace.

For Miss Grace and I had a special relationship. She even asked me if I would like to spend the night with her every now and then. I must have been around ten years old then. Of course I said yes, and whenever she wanted to have me over, she would write a note for me to take home to my mother. And the next day when I went to school, I took a little brown paper bag with an extra set of clothes in it, so that I could stay over with Miss Grace.

Those were some of the best evenings of my life. After school was out, Miss Grace and I would walk back to her little rooms in the boardinghouse. It was only a few blocks from the school, not the six miles I had to walk from my house, and we would just talk and laugh all the way. She was always carrying a huge stack of books, and she gave me a stack of papers to carry. We would walk down the streets just laughing, and all the men would stop to look at her. I'm sure they were wondering, "Now what is that beautiful lady doing with that ugly child?" But I didn't care, and Miss Grace probably didn't even notice.

Whatever I told her I wanted for supper, I would get it. We cooked the food together, and then after supper I would help her grade the papers from that day's class. If I didn't know the answers myself, she never scolded me for grading wrong. She would just say little things like, "Well, think about it, Oral, count it out to yourself. Is that really the answer you want to say is right?"

And then, when it was time for bed, I got my own bed in my own room. I never had anything like that at home! So you can understand how I just felt like the most special person on earth around Miss Grace. Those nights always flew by. I was always sad to wake up in the morning.

When I did go back home, I would be on a high from everything Miss Grace had done and said. She was all I could talk about. It must have offended my mother in some sense, to see her child—this child who loved her more than anything—come in and go on and on about this other woman. It's a sign of my mother's respect for teachers that she never said anything about it.

THE PROMISE

I have put Miss Grace up there with my mother in terms of what she meant to me as a child growing up in the South. She was a true role model, and not just because she was so gracious and sweet. She taught me more than any other teacher I've had. I don't even remember the names of my other schoolteachers, but I've been trying to look up Miss Grace for years. I heard she married a mean man who beat her, and I hope that's not the case. If so, it speaks to his weakness rather than hers.

Miss Grace showed me that education can take you places, even if you're a woman. There were two facts about her that were fascinating to me—she came from somewhere else, and she had gone to college. The fact that she had left her hometown meant that maybe I could get out of my hometown, too.

And the fact that she had been to college meant that she could become a teacher. That was the highest ambition a mother could have for her daughter back then, to become a teacher or a nurse. I believe my mother wanted me to be a teacher, and surely the respect she showed for Miss Grace was an incentive to me. But as powerful as that incentive was, I believe that it was those two facts together that really struck me. She had left her hometown *and* she had gotten her education. I started thinking even then about whether those two facts were correlated. Could getting an education help *me* leave home? What else could it do? I truly believe that having Miss Grace as a teacher shaped my life. She's a big part of the reason why I started down the path I've followed to this day.

The second thing that started me down the path I've followed to this day is what happened to my four eldest brothers on a Saturday night in 1955. I must have been about nine years old.

My four eldest brothers are all just one year apart in age. My mother had her first four kids one right after the other — in 1927, '28, '29, and '30. Since they were all boys, and so close in age, they grew up together as close as any siblings can be. Every chore they did, they did together. Every bit of cotton they picked, they picked standing side by side in the rows. And everywhere they went, they went together. So of course when they went out on this particular Saturday night, they went to the local nightclub, or "juke," together. It's very important to know that my brothers went to the juke on Saturday nights, but they went to the juke because there was nowhere else for black people to go. They weren't interested in some of the nasty business that happened in those jukes, and they certainly weren't interested in drinking. My daddy didn't allow that.

CQ, the youngest of the four, would have been the driver. I wouldn't have paid too much attention to them when they left the house that night. Like I said, they went out every Saturday night. But I certainly remember what happened when they came back to the house that night. Somebody must have woken me up, because it was *that* bad.

My four brothers . . . it's difficult for me to even describe it because they don't beat people like that anymore. They just don't. There was blood everywhere. I mean, CQ's face was beaten so badly that both of his eyes were closed. My other brothers looked like they had swallowed golf balls. Everyone was spitting blood. There were broken bones, broken noses, broken teeth . . . and we didn't know *what* might be broken inside. They couldn't even walk. Somehow, they managed to drive home. God was obviously protecting them on that drive home, because CQ couldn't see and the other ones had lost some of their sight, too, thanks to broken noses and swollen eyes and all the rest of it. They made it home, and then one of them had to crawl to the house. He had to *crawl!* That's how bad it was.

We learned later that someone in town had seen the beating. This person actually followed my brothers home in his truck, because he was positive that my brothers were not going to live long enough to get home. Then he turned off the road before our house. Now, I don't know why this person didn't jump in to try and stop the beating—I'm sure my brothers would have appreciated that a little bit more—but that should give you an idea of how serious this was. My father didn't know if they were going to live through the night.

But they did. They lived through that night and the next night, and with a whole lot of sacrifice on our parts they managed to begin healing. It took months. You're talking about broken bones and faces, not to mention all the damage we didn't know about. Then there's the psychological factor. Because you see, it wasn't just anybody who was responsible for beating my brothers this way. It was Batesville's white sheriff, Ross Darby. Ross Darby had a reputation for abusing black people whenever he could get away with it, and because segregation was the way that it was, he could *always* get away with it. No one would dare stand up to him, because that meant that your whole family could be killed.

That includes my brothers. I can't imagine what they must have gone through, knowing the man who beat them but

knowing they couldn't beat him back. It's such a shame because I know that my four brothers could have torn him up.

Well, they couldn't beat him back with their fists, anyway.
But somebody—and to this day we don't know who this person was—had a suggestion for how we could beat Ross Darby
another way.

Now, there's always been someone like this mysterious individual in every black village and community. There were
probably more of them back then, especially in the South, than
there are now. I'm talking about the person who gets mad. Not
angry. Not frustrated. Not weary. Every black person in the
South was all of those things! I'm talking about somebody
who gets *mad*. Somebody who decides that they're going to
defy the odds, they're not going to take anymore, they're going to stand up and rebel in some sort of way. And in the South
it was usually an underhanded way, because rebelling openly
would get you shot in an instant. During slavery it was the sort
of person who would poison the master's food, and during my
childhood it was the sort of person who secretly called the
NAACP.

To this day I would love to know who did it. It certainly
wasn't my parents. They were too busy trying to hold the crop
together without the help of my four brothers, and too worried
about what had happened, to get mad. But somebody got mad,
and he or she got word to Robert Miles and the NAACP in
Chicago.

We never knew who called the NAACP, but we certainly
knew when they came into town. Everybody knew. All of the
South is a small town, really, and when someone from out of
town comes in—especially folks from the North, and *especially*

troublemakers like the NAACP—the whole town knows in a matter of minutes. So we knew the NAACP men were coming to see us long before they got to our house. And you can be sure that the white folks in town knew, too.

Well, they pulled up, and it was one of the most beautiful sights I have ever seen. My first memory is of hearing somebody say, "Who is that flying?" There were nothing but dirt roads in the Vance Bottom, and we could see the dust from the road starting to stir up already, even though no car had driven up yet. Then the dust flew more and more, like a little tornado in the Vance Bottom, and all of a sudden it started to part in the middle. I mean, to me it was like Moses was holding his staff out over the water! The dust was just parting, parting, parting, to let this big blue and white car through. They pulled that car up in front of our house, and even though it's been such a long time I can still remember every move they made. They stopped the car, and as the dust started to settle down again all four doors of the car opened at the same time.

So all the doors of the car pop open at the same time, and four of these fine men stand up and get out. I thought they would close all four doors at the same time too, but there was a fifth man in the backseat who needed to get out, so I guess they hadn't figured out how to do that yet. Five men, all of them in these staunch suits. People didn't wear suits in Batesville, even the white people. It just wasn't done. This was the middle of the week, too, and in the middle of the week nobody in our little farming town, black or white, rich or poor, wore decent clothes.

But that rule didn't apply to our heroes from the NAACP. They walked up to the porch wearing suits, and Stetson hats, and alligator shoes! I thought they were from another planet. And they were gentlemen. They asked politely if they might be able to see Mr. Walter Bivins.

Somebody must have gone to fetch my father—it certainly wasn't me, I couldn't move. I was practically paralyzed sitting there watching these five men. But somebody went into the field and told my father that he had some visitors. And when Daddy appeared I came to my senses. I was still a well-behaved child, even if I asked too many questions. If you grew up in the South, you'll know that well-behaved children disappear when adults start talking. But I was going to know what was going on that day, I can tell you that. So when everyone else went to the back of the house like we were supposed to, I went right around the back of the house and slipped under the porch.

I had a serious interest in this, you see. Even then I loved my brother CQ more than anything in the world, and I was just furious that he had been beaten to a pulp. I didn't know anything about the mission of the NAACP at that age. I just knew that white folks didn't like them at all, and that was good enough for me. That probably meant they could do something about the men who had beaten up CQ.

They exchanged their pleasantries, and then they started talking about what had happened. I don't remember exactly what my father said to them about the beating, but I can remember what Robert Miles's response was. He said to my father, "Mr. Walter, you have a case. They're saying in town that the reason all of your sons were beaten is because all of them were drunk."

This may not seem like much of a factor to hang a case on,

but back then everybody knew who you were and what you did. Everyone always knew who was sleeping with so-and-so's wife, and who had lost everything gambling on horses, and all the rest of it. And they'd smile real big in your face and talk about it behind your back, but you can be assured that no one had secrets in the South. Batesville was no different. Everybody in town, for example, knew that the Bivins boys did not drink. Everybody knew that, and everybody knew *why* they didn't drink—because my father wouldn't have it. But Ross Darby had spread the rumor that he had beat my brothers because they were drunk, and in their drunkenness they had tried to do something to him.

In the opinion of Robert Miles and the NAACP, this was all my father needed to pursue a case against Ross Darby. Underneath the porch, I was listening to this and getting excited. I was thinking that my brothers would finally have their revenge. Listening to all of this talk about a lawsuit and a court case I was getting really excited, thinking that we were finally going to get Ross Darby. But of course I was only eight or nine years old, and I wasn't really aware of what the consequences might be. So I was floored when I heard my father say, "We can't do it."

My father said, "We can't do it. You see, you get to go back to Chicago, but my family has to stay here. And the minute you leave, the white people uptown will walk on down to the Bottom one night and they will kill my whole family."

I don't know what got into me, but I jumped up onto the porch. In that second of surprise I had, I faced the adults and I yelled, "I don't care! I wish they would kill you, because you're dead anyway!"

Ooh, my mama slapped me so hard! And then I ran away before anything else could happen, because of course by this point I had come to my senses. That was a funny moment, because I wasn't the sort of child who talked back to my parents, especially in front of company. But that particular decision had hurt me to my heart. It was like I was seeing my life get back in that car and drive to Chicago! Not only that, but that meant there would be no revenge for my brothers. It was the combination of those two things that pushed me onto that porch with such a shout.

When I was older, my mother asked me why I did it. She said, "Oral Lee, why'd you say such hurtful things to your daddy? And in front of all those men?" And I told her the answer was simple. I could not believe what my daddy had done. You know, when you're a child lots of things your parents do may seem wrong to you, but usually you have enough sense to understand their actions, even if you don't agree with them. Well, that was the situation I was in under that porch. You can believe that I went through it under there, scratching my head, listening to my father's explanations, listening to Robert Miles and the NAACP, listening to them try and talk my father into a lawsuit. In the end, after I tried to get everything sorted out in my head, after I tried to understand why my father was making the decision he had made—well, it was simple. I couldn't even figure out why my father was saying such things. To me there was no other logical action except what the NAACP men were saying!

"Why wouldn't he stand up?" That's the response I gave my mother. And she would just shake her head and say, "But you know how things were then, Oral Lee." We went round and round about it for years, long after I was grown. I told her that I felt it was 100 percent wrong. My brothers had not done anything to anyone. They did not deserve that beating. And somebody needed to stop Ross Darby. I mean, he did *everything*. He killed people, he raped women, he walked into people's houses and started fighting them there, *in their own homes*—someone needed to stop this man. "Sure," said my mother. "I'm with you, Oral Lee. Somebody needed to stop him. But why did that somebody have to be us?" "Well, why shouldn't it?" I asked her. That's how it went, until we were both so worn out that we were laughing. We could laugh about it then, but it was terrible. It was truly terrible. And in many ways I don't think I've ever gotten over my father's decision not to sue that man. It was the first time in my life that I came face to face with injustice, and it was the first time I realized that sometimes people are helpless in the face of it.

Because of that incident, I've always determined to be as active as I could be in the face of injustice. That includes racial injustice, economic injustice, and it *definitely* includes educational injustice.

The incident with Ross Darby crushed my brothers in some ways, too. Within two years of that beating, they had all left Mississippi. The eldest, Perry, got married and moved to Memphis. Another brother, Alvin, went to St. Louis and was found dead a few years later in mysterious circumstances. And EQ and CQ both joined the army, served for many years, and decided to settle where they were discharged—California's Bay Area.

EQ and CQ were, hands down, my favorite brothers. CQ and I always had a very special relationship, dating back to childhood. He was a fighter just like I was. He once told me that he knew he had to get out of Mississippi after that incident, because otherwise he would have hauled off and shot Ross Darby. That was just how I felt, and I think it was best that both of us left when we did. As for EQ, he was more than ten years older than I was, so I didn't really get to know him until we got older. But then we became very close, and I came to regard him as the kindest man I've ever met.

These two men are the reason that I decided to move to California. I never would have thought of it on my own. After I turned eighteen and graduated from high school, I went right to work in Newburgh, New York. I worked at a handbag factory and earned about a dollar an hour. It wasn't a lot of money, but it was more than I could have made in Mississippi, so I just plugged along. But CQ and EQ kept telling me about how wonderful it was in Oakland, California.

"The temperature is perfect here all the time," they told me. "And we've got good jobs at a construction company—much better than we could've gotten in Mississippi. Pretty soon we're going to buy our own houses, and they're going to have big lawns and plenty of space."

They told me things like that, knowing that I was living in a cramped apartment in New York, under skies that always seemed to be gray. So when CQ bought his house and offered to let me live with him if I decided to come to California, I jumped at the chance. I bought a ticket on a Greyhound bus and arrived in California when I was twenty years old.

When I first moved there, I thought Oakland was heaven. Part of it is just that I'm from the South, and I'm used to big open spaces and pretty skies. I like having a little space between me and my neighbor, for a garden or whatever. We had all that in Mississippi, but there were also those little problems of poverty and segregation. In New York there was opportunity, but it was so urban that it was stifling. In California there was opportunity, sunshine, *and* wide open spaces to breathe. I thought I'd finally found the best of both worlds.

Back then, Oakland didn't look the way it does now. People kept their lawns manicured. The streets were lined with trees. The homes, even the small ones, were well-loved and well-maintained. East Oakland was full of department stores and banks and places for people to meet their neighbors and have a nice cup of coffee together. All the crime came later. All the drugs, all the killing . . . that wasn't going on back then. When I arrived in 1962 the city was calm and prosperous. And at night you could look up and see the stars opening up in front of you like you were on the way to the moon.

There was plenty of opportunity in Oakland, too, if you were willing to work hard. With CQ's financial help, I went to cosmetology school and became a hairdresser. As soon as I got a job, I moved out of CQ's house and found an apartment with my little sister, Mary. I wasn't the only family member who was tempted by the promise of California. Over the years, all of my siblings moved to Oakland. CQ and EQ helped all of them find work and housing. Eventually, when my mother realized that none of us were coming back—it didn't take any of us long to get used to running water and peaceful neighborhoods—she moved too.

Young, happy, and employed, I did what was common in those days: I got married. Today I warn my adopted girls to avoid the mistake that I made and make sure that they get their college degrees before they get married. I married my first husband when I was far too young, and by the time I was twenty-four I had three daughters, Michelle, Lynn, and Phyllis.

Then I got divorced. And there I was, not quite thirty, with three daughters and no husband. George never offered me a penny of child support, not that I would've taken it if he had. But it's no easy job being a mother even when you've got a supportive husband, and being a single mother is more work than any woman ever imagines.

I tell my adopted kids to wait until after they've got their education to get married, and then wait until they're forty to have kids. They all laugh at me, but I'm not joking. I tell them to look at their own parents, and to think about what they went through trying to support them.

I've been in the same place that their mothers have—broke, alone, and without any support from the father of my children. And I can speak from experience that it's hard to feed and educate your kids at the same time. I remember so many impossible days when I was raising my three daughters alone. I left the house at seven-thirty in the morning, worked my three jobs, and then got home at ten o'clock at night. If the girls had been in school during those years, would I have had the energy to stay up and check their homework? I don't think so.

So I don't judge poor parents or parents who are depending on welfare, trying to raise five kids on jobs that pay $7 an hour. I don't ask about why they don't supervise their kids the way that they should, because I've been there. And when that was my life, it was overwhelming. There were days when I wanted to give up, and I know that some parents *do* give up. That's why I could never get angry at the parents of my adopted kids when they didn't show up at events. I got frustrated, yes, but then I would tell myself: *Oral Lee, you've been there. Maybe today they just couldn't make it out of the house one more time. And besides, you didn't adopt the parents. You adopted the kids. So be there for them when their parents can't be.*

I was a lucky single mom, way luckier than most. I had my whole extended family around me. My mother lived right down the street from me, and I had eight brothers and sisters within a five-mile radius who I could lean on. They saved me many, many times.

I was also fortunate that my second husband was a wonderful man and a great father. I won't say much about my first husband, George—but Joe Brown was a good, good man. His family is also from Batesville, and he was a good friend of my brother CQ. That's how we got to know each other. We started dating about four years after my divorce. I was reluctant at first, but I found, to my surprise, that Joe Brown was the nicest man I was ever going to meet. In all the years that we were married, we never had a fight. He thought I was the best thing that ever happened to him.

The most amazing thing about Joe was the way he behaved as a father. I've seen a lot of situations where stepchildren are made to feel like second-class citizens—that didn't happen in our house. As far as my daughters were concerned, their daddy was Joe Brown. That's what they called him, and that's how he acted. He took them to and from school, helped them with their homework, guided them through all the headaches that come with adolescence—he did all of it. We were such a happy family while the girls were growing up.

And I would like to say that our happiness continued all the way through up to the present day, but you know, God has plans for all of us that we can't anticipate. And his plan for my family was that we needed to learn how to get on without someone. I lost my eldest daughter, Michelle, in 1977. She had an epileptic seizure and swallowed her tongue.

Now, I love all three of my daughters. They all have different personalities, which is one of the great joys and wonders of having children. My youngest child, Phyllis, is ambitious and headstrong. It's always been her way or no way, ever since she was a child. She's very determined and focused, and she would never accept anything for herself but success. I admire her for that—she's got a lot of her mother in her. Lynn, the middle child, is calmer and more easygoing. She takes the world as it comes, and she's a lot more likely to listen to other people for input before she makes a decision. She's also a shopaholic, but I can't single her out for that because all my girls love to shop and their mother does too!

But Michelle always had something special about her. She was a beautiful girl, and I'm not just saying that because she was mine. She loved the fact that people used to stop her and tell her how lovely she was, but she wasn't a snob. She was warm and loving toward other people, but she was a little dreamy. It was almost as if she had a special space around her that made people want to be around her even more.

Michelle had suffered from seizures ever since she was about a year old, and none of the doctors knew what was wrong with her. They kept her on medications until she was about ten years old, and then they figured that she had grown out of the seizures. I've learned since her death that once a person has even a single seizure, she is at risk for the rest of her life. She should never have been taken off those medications.

I wasn't there when Michelle died. I wish to God I had been. She had asked to spend the night at her Aunt Willie Bea's house, which was a couple of miles away from our house in East Oakland. I thought it was a bit strange, because she had never asked to spend the night before, but I said of course. And around eleven o'clock at night I got a call from Willie Bea that was nothing but a voice screaming. Of course I rushed over there, thinking that there was something wrong with Willie Bea, and as soon as I walked in the door two hospital orderlies gave me a shot to sedate me. I never even got to see my daughter again.

There's nothing anyone can say to you when you lose a child. When anyone who's close to you dies, it's painful, but when your own child dies it's more than that. Mothers aren't supposed to bury their children. It goes against everything we feel about having kids and living our lives.

Michelle's death pulled my family together. We were closer than ever after that, although her sisters still can't talk about her death. I can also say that God wants the sweetest and the best people on this earth earlier than He wants the rest of us, which is why the people who are most precious to us always seem to die too soon. I do believe that He knows what He's doing and there's a reason why He chose Michelle. He must have known that He just let her out of heaven a little bit too quick, and it was high time that He corrected that oversight. I suppose if you think about it that way, He was kind to let me keep her on this earth for as long as He did.

After her death, my whole family started thinking about what we could do to make our lives on this earth more meaningful. One of the things I decided to do was fulfill some of my long-standing goals, like getting a college education. I had always wanted to go to college, but I just had never had the money or the time. But after Michelle's death, I realized that my own time on this earth is limited, and I went about doing some of the things I'd always said I would do.

Even with all my determination, I still might not have had the opportunity to go to college if I hadn't been fortunate enough to work for Blue Cross Health Insurance. I started there as a file clerk in the late 1960s, moving up through the ranks until I was ready to apply for the job of finance manager. But just as I was about to do that, I got a call from the head of human resources. He said that the decision had just come through that a college degree was required for applicants for the job of finance manager, and while Blue Cross fully intended to give me the position, they would like to know if I might be willing to go back to school.

"I'd love to," I said. "But like a lot of things I'd love to do, school is something I can't afford." I meant it, too. It was the late 1970s, and I was making around $29,000 a year. That was a lot of money to me—certainly more than I'd ever expected to make—but I still had children to support. The family had Joe's income, too, but we weren't rich by any stretch of the imagination. And from what I knew about the cost of tuition— not to mention the cost of time—I'd need to earn a whole lot more money in order to go back to school.

To my surprise, the man from human resources explained that Blue Cross had a tuition program for their employees.

They would be willing to pay 80 percent of my tuition costs if I studied for a degree that was relevant to my position. "We'll support you," he said. "You've been one of our best employees, and we'll give you flexible hours and do whatever else we have to do."

Well, he didn't need to ask me twice. It had always been a dream of mine to go to college, and now that I had my chance, I didn't hesitate. I signed up for Blue Cross's tuition program and immediately began researching different schools and programs. Eventually, I went to the University of San Francisco and earned my bachelor's in Human Resources. I worked during the day and went to school at night, and it was not easy. I honestly believed that I only made it for two reasons: my mother lived right down the street, and I had a supportive husband. But how many people can say that? And even with all that help, I feel like I barely saw either my mother or my husband, much less my daughters, for the five and a half years that it took me to get my degree.

People are often amazed when they learn that I didn't get my degree until I was in my forties. It's true: when I made my promise to put my babies through college, I had barely graduated myself. In many ways the struggles I went through trying to get my own degree motivated me to make sure that they wouldn't have to experience the same thing.

I worked at Blue Cross until 1983. I can say without arrogance that the human resources manager was right about me: I was one of the best employees Blue Cross has ever had. Now, I say that not only because I've always wanted to be the best at everything I've ever done, but also because of what I did for the company. While I was working there, it was my opinion that everyone in the world needed Blue Cross's health insurance *and* that they needed to pay their premiums on time. I wouldn't say that I got everyone in the world to agree with my opinion, but I came awfully close: over the course of my eighteen years of employment for Blue Cross, I put more than $2 billion in the bank for them.

In the end, though, I just got tired. After I quit, I had an exit interview with five different people—one of them happened to be Beverly Clack, the vice president of the company. She offered me everything she could think of to get me to stay. When that didn't work, she let me go with the understanding that as long as Blue Cross had one employee who needed a supervisor, Oral Lee Brown had a job. I thanked them from the bottom of my heart, and then I moved on. It was time for the next challenge.

I didn't exactly go looking for my next career—I like to say that it found me. I was walking down Lyndhurst Street in Oakland, minding my own business, when I saw a For Sale sign in front of a house. Joe, the girls, and I had been thinking about moving into a bigger place, and I liked the look of this one. So I called the realtors in charge of the sale, a group called Lowe Realty.

"Are you responsible for a house on Lyndhurst Street?" I asked the man who picked up the phone.

"And hello to you, too," he said, and he sounded amused. "My name's Mr. Walls, and yes, we are in charge of a house on Lyndhurst Street. Are you interested?"

That's how my friendship with Mr. Walls—a friendship that lasted for the next twenty years—began. He thought there was something special about me immediately. By the time we

finished our first phone conversation, I had confessed to him
that I loved houses and had always wanted to work in real estate, and he had extracted a promise from me to come down to
Lowe Realty's offices and talk to him and his partners. They
were looking for a new employee, he told me, and perhaps I'd
be a good fit.

Well, if you used any objective standards, I certainly didn't
fit into Lowe Realty. It was a real estate group run by twenty
older gentlemen, all of them originally from the South. And
while I liked the owners instantly—they carried themselves in
an old-fashioned, gentlemanly way that reminded me of my father—I wasn't sure where I would fit into their company, and
I wasn't sure if I wanted to get into real estate at that time. If
I sign up to do anything, I'm going to put all of my heart and
soul into it, and I knew that if I signed up to do real estate, I
would try to sell every house in Oakland!

That was not going to be an easy task, not by any stretch
of the imagination. Oakland had changed since I arrived there,
and not for the better. By the 1980s Oakland was going
straight to hell. When I first moved there in the 1960s, everything a resident could possibly need, from banks to supermar-
kets to department stores, was on East 14th Street, which
is now called International Boulevard. Fifteen years later
the whole street was full of abandoned storefronts and shelled-
out buildings. It's been twenty years since, and even the city
government people downtown, who have tried all kinds of "urban renewal" plans, haven't been able to bring businesses
back.

In 1980 the city's unemployment rate was nearly 20 percent.
Forty-six percent of the city's residents over the age of twenty-

five didn't have high school diplomas. White people, who were nearly 60 percent of the population in 1970, made up only 37 percent of the population in 1980. They ran and they ran fast, as soon as the city got its first black mayor in 1977. And when they left, businesses left, and when businesses leave, there goes your tax base. Without a tax base, the only things left in your city are problems, and believe me, Oakland had plenty of those. Violent crime became a way of life, especially when crack cocaine hit the streets in the late 1980s. That drug in particular is responsible for what happened to this community, because people were willing to do anything for it. It broke my heart to watch Oakland spiral downhill like that, because when I moved here I thought it was the most beautiful place in the world. And I still love Oakland.

That was my environment now, but perhaps real estate could offer a way to improve it. I thought that I could contribute to the community by selling houses to hardworking people who felt invested in Oakland, despite all of its problems. That was Lowe Realty's specialty, low- and medium-income housing. It's not the sort of brokerage that will earn you a lot of respect or a lot of money. But I loved the idea that I could help people who had struggled all of their lives to get a piece of the American Dream. And I loved the fact that we were making it happen in Oakland. "I'm here to help you build a better neighborhood," I told my clients.

The men who ran Lowe Realty were thrilled that I took to real estate so naturally. We all got along so well that when it came time for them to sell the business and retire, they offered it to me. I'll never know why they gave me such an opportunity—all twenty of them had grown children who might have

liked the chance—but I took it, and in 1985 I was happily settled, with my very own real estate company.

I thought that was going to be my life until retirement. I had
never been directly involved in community activism because
I've always preferred to make a difference in quiet ways—
mostly by living an example of hard work and discipline.

Besides, my plate was full to the brim. Running a business
is difficult and time-consuming—there were always problem-
atic houses to deal with or new employees to train. My daughters were getting ready to go to college, so I was scraping
together the money to pay for that. And of course, there was
the stress of living in a city that was full of crackheads killing
each other on the streets. So I certainly wasn't planning to
take on any additional responsibilities on that day in 1987
when I walked over to the grocery store on 94th Avenue to
pick up a packet of Spanish peanuts and a Pepsi.

2

How I Saved the Money

All of this brings us up to December 1987. Somehow, I had gone from being a regular old realtor, a woman who'd had her fair share of tribulations and maybe more than her share of blessings too, to a woman on the run from flashbulbs and media attention.

❧

The next couple of weeks after I decided to adopt the first-grade class were a whirlwind of meetings with parents and education supervisors. Everyone I met with seemed impressed that I was willing to make such a major commitment to these children, especially such a major financial commitment. I didn't talk too much about money, but they must have known that I wasn't rich. "It's amazing that you're willing to make sacrifices for these children," they said. I thanked them and said it wouldn't be a sacrifice, because whenever you give up something to help others you don't really lose anything. That's my opinion, anyway. But apparently it's not one that's shared by many people in this world, or at least not enough people in the world to make my story less than special. Because I really didn't realize how impressed those members of the board of education were until about a month after I first talked to the principal, Mrs. Peeks, about adopting the class. One of the board members went to his boss, Don Peralta, who was an Alameda County supervisor, and told him about me.

"What?" said Mr. Peralta. "Does anybody know about this?" And that's how it happened that one afternoon I tried to walk into my real estate office and was attacked by cameras and reporters.

"How are you going to do it, Mrs. Brown?" they shouted. "Where's the money going to come from?" And then the flashbulbs started going off, and I turned and ran out of my office. I got into my car and started driving. Some of the reporters were in hot pursuit, but they gave up after it became obvious that I wasn't going to stop. I kept driving all the way down to the Alameda pier. When I got there, I parked the car, turned off the engine, and spent the next half-hour trying to get my breath back.

You see, I've never wanted any publicity for my efforts with these kids. As far as I was concerned, the mission I was undertaking didn't warrant any special attention at all. Maybe some emotional support from the public would have been nice. Some financial support *certainly* would've been nice. But I was actually hurt that the first time I met with the media—yes, I did eventually stop hiding from them and agree to do some interviews—they were very skeptical.

Everybody's first question was, "Do you really think you can do it?" Well, of course I *knew* I could do it! If not, I wouldn't have said that I could in the first place. Now, granted, I didn't know what I was getting into when I made my promise to Mrs. Peeks and the class of children that she selected for me. I didn't know I was going to be buying food and clothes for them when they didn't have any at home. I didn't know that I was going to be "on-call" for these kids every day up until the present. I certainly didn't know that I would be setting up a foundation and a million and one projects to help them make it through school. But once I say I'm going to do something, you can be sure that I'm going to do it. No matter what it takes.

There was even one reporter who asked me a question that just hurt me to my heart. I've never forgotten it. He was a reporter with Channel 5, a local news station here in Oakland, and after I had answered everybody else's questions he walked up to me and asked if he could have a word with me away from the cameras. We stepped aside, and he said to me quietly, "Now, come on, Mrs. Brown. Off the record, tell me the truth. How many of them do you really think will graduate from high school?"

My mouth fell open. I was furious. This man assumed that just because the kids at Brookfield were poor, and just because they came from a neighborhood that was crippled by poverty and drugs and everything else, that they were *inevitably* going to turn out to be useless—I ran over to his cameraman and told him to come over to where the reporter and I were standing. And for the first and last time in my life I grabbed the reporter's microphone and stood in front of that camera by my own choice.

"No, you get this on the record," I said. "You can believe this—every single one of these kids will graduate from high school."

And in fact they did, so thank God I didn't prove that reporter right! But that experience let me know what I was going to be facing throughout my time with these kids—a lot of suspicion, skepticism, and doubt, and very little support. I'm glad I wasn't aware of such feelings when we started the adoption process, which we had done several weeks before the media caught on.

After the board of education had completed all their checks into my background, Mrs. Peeks told me that she had selected Carrie Waters's first-grade class. "Mrs. Waters is an excellent teacher, and she'll give you a lot of support for what you're trying to do," Mrs. Peeks said. As a bonus, Mrs. Waters could also teach the second grade, so if things went well the first year, it was possible that my students could stay with her.

"Great," I said. "What's next?"

The next step was to let all the parents of the twenty-three children in the class know what I wanted to do. Mrs. Peeks and I drafted a letter that was sent to all of them. In the letter we asked them to attend a special mandatory meeting. At that meeting, the letter said, the parents would get an opportunity to meet me and learn about the project I was proposing for their children.

I brought the associate reverend of my church, Frank Gilbert, to that first meeting with all the parents. I had known Frank for at least ten years and had a tremendous amount of respect for him. He was one of the few people I had spoken to, by choice that is, about my decision to adopt the class.

"That's God's work, Oral," he had said. "You're doing a great thing." That made me feel so good that I asked him to come along to my first meeting with the parents. I figured he could vouch for my character if any of the parents were suspicious about what I wanted with their children. I also brought him along for emotional support, because I was scared stiff.

Fortunately, the meeting went well. First of all, all the parents showed up. That wasn't to happen very many other times in the course of my dealings with the kids, but I was very happy that we'd gotten off to a positive start. Most of them were single mothers—there were only four fathers still in the households of the twenty-three kids when I started the program. (There were only two by the time they graduated from high school.) There were also quite a few grandparents who were raising these kids.

Mrs. Peeks introduced me and said a few words about what I wanted to do with the students, emphasizing what a great opportunity this was for the children. Then I got up and spoke, explaining what at the time I thought I meant by "adoption": that I was planning to spend several hours a week with their children at school, and save $10,000 a year for their college education.

Everyone was enthusiastic; everyone announced their intention to help. But—and I don't say this to disparage the parents—I remember asking them, "How many of you have already started saving for your child to go to college?" And I remember that not a single hand went up.

Well, that was a strong hint about what I was getting myself into, and maybe that's why I sat in my car in the parking lot of the school for at least thirty minutes after the meeting was over, shaking uncontrollably. I mean, my hands were shaking so badly that I literally couldn't put the key in the ignition. And after about a half-hour of trying I started to laugh at myself. "Is this going to be a habit, Mrs. Brown?" I said to myself as I sat there. "Come on now, it's not that bad. You'll figure out what you're doing eventually. But you can't figure anything out if you keep hanging out in this car. Now get your act together." With that, I managed to fit the key into the ignition. A couple of minutes later I managed to turn it on. And finally I found the focus to put the car in gear and drive away.

⚭

At that point I still hadn't told my husband or anyone in my family except my brother EQ. I wanted to make sure that I had everything in order, every *t* crossed and *i* dotted, before I came to them with my argument about why I had decided to do this and why they ought to support me. (Of course, then the media found out, so I had to rush home and tell them before they read it in the morning paper. Their response, to put it mildly, was shock.) There were a number of things I wanted to complete before telling my family what I had done, and tops on that list was setting up a trust account for the kids' education. I had already decided that I wanted Frank Gilbert to be a trustee for the account with me, and after working with her for a little while I decided to ask Mrs. Peeks as well.

A lot of people ask me how I managed to come up with $240,000 for the kids' education. The answer is simple: I set the account up in such a way that I wasn't allowed to touch it! You see, I'm no financial expert. I don't know anything about Wall Street, never learned a thing about stocks or bonds or all the ways those men in suits make their millions. I was never trying to make millions. I was trying to send these kids to school. And for that, I figured I only needed to know two things: One, we couldn't afford to lose any of the money; two, I had to make sure that none of the money was being used for anything but the kids' education.

Number one is the reason why I never put the money into stocks. Oh, sure, I got calls from Charles Schwab and Merrill Lynch and all those big investment banks. They all figured that they could do better with my money than I could, and they very well may have been right. But as soon as I made my promise, that money was no longer mine. I couldn't afford to take any risks with it. And the one thing I know about the stock market is that there is risk involved. I could not face the heartbreak of walking into some investor's office in twelve years' time and hearing, "Well, the bottom of the stock market's fallen out and now your kids won't have enough money to go to school." So I decided to sacrifice the potential of higher gains for security, and I went with an option I knew about from real estate: trust accounts.

You can set up a trust account at just about any bank in this country. You get a much higher interest rate than with savings accounts or money market accounts, because you agree to leave the principal with the bank for a period of years. In my case, I made an arrangement with the bank that no one was to touch the money until 1999, and that even then, the money was only to go to a college or an institution of higher learning.

With those two conditions, as well as my promise to invest $10,000 a year, I managed to get an interest rate of about 9 percent a year, which is pretty good. It's not the stock market—they say that long-term, the stock market averages a return of between 10 and 15 percent—but I knew that if the stock market lost value, as it always does, I wouldn't have to be worried. As it happened, I would've just missed the cut-off date if I'd invested that money in stocks: the stock market was flying as high as a bird in 1999 and then crashed in 2000. So I may have missed out on some money, but I saved myself a whole lot of stress.

If parents are looking to save money for their kids' education, I can recommend trust accounts as a good way to do it. The only thing about trust accounts is that you have to start early, like as soon as your child is born! I was bowled over when I found out that none of those parents had started saving for college. I started saving for my own kids' college education as soon as they were born. I didn't have tons of money to save for them, but what I did save I just put in an account with a good long-term interest rate, and over the years it added up.

That's all you have to do, really. You have to start saving early if you want to get the benefits, because with the right bank and the right account, the interest on your money compounds every year. That's how you get your money to go a lot further than it would if you were just putting it in a regular old bank savings account.

"But how am I supposed to do that?" I've heard parents ask me. "I don't know what you did or how you did it, Oral, but I can barely make ends meet every month." I'm sympathetic to that argument. I know what it's like to be poor. But no matter how poor you are, you can still save something. I certainly wasn't rich when I started saving for these kids either, I was making about $45,000, but I managed to save $10,000 a year. I may have had to give up a couple of restaurant dinners and a few shopping trips to Macy's, but you know what? I really didn't miss anything that I had to give up in order to save that money. And whoever you are, no matter how poor you are, I'm sure that you're spending money on something that wouldn't really be missed if you had to give it up to save for your kids' education. Maybe it's that big color TV. Or maybe it's the car that you want to lease, the one that sucks up too much gas anyway. Or maybe it's just the bag of Fritos that you buy every week at the supermarket or that fancy coffee you buy every day—I'm sure you can find *something*. And every little bit helps.

What I decided was this: there were two months I wasn't going to give up spending my usual budget on. Those two months were December, because I love the Christmas holidays, and February, which is the month of my birthday. So that meant the other ten months out of the year I had to come up with $1,000 in savings. Ten months a year, as soon as I got paid, the first thing I did was walk over to Home Savings Bank and deposit $1,000 in the trust account. Without fail. Before I paid any bills or even went shopping for groceries. I figured that was the only way that money would actually get in the bank, and whenever I've spoken to other people who are good at saving money, they do the same thing too. Get that money in a savings account before you can even look at it or know that it's there, is what they say. And now that banks have direct deposit and all sorts of electronic strategies to help you get your money in separate accounts, it's easier than ever to save.

I was in for a surprise when I started saving, though. One of the big benefits that I was counting on was the ability to write my donations to the kids' trust account off on my taxes. I mean, I had given $10,000 to what was essentially a charitable cause, even if it wasn't a traditional charity. So in 1988, after the first year I'd contributed $10,000 to the kids, I wrote off $10,000 for charitable contributions. Well, maybe the Internal Revenue Service was suspicious since I didn't have receipts for that money, because they sent me a letter in response. And in this letter they explained to me that if I wanted to claim $10,000 in charitable contributions for these kids' educations, I had to find matching funds in order for it to be valid as a tax write-off.

Well, that got me scratching my head. Matching funds? What could I do, walk up to someone and ask them to hand me $10,000 to match a contribution I was making for the children's education? Half the reason why I was saving the money was because no one else was willing to do it!

The only way I could think of to get matching funds was to ask for donations in return for some sort of service, whether it was holding a car wash or a bake sale or arranging for the kids to raise money by running a marathon. But putting aside the very large question of the extra time and effort on my part that such things required, my biggest question was a simple one: Would we be able to get enough money?

I spoke to a good friend of mine, who helps me with my taxes and who eventually came to sit on the board of my foundation, about the situation. "How am I going to do this?" I asked. She didn't have any suggestions about fund-raisers, but she did bring up one very important point: when people donate money to a cause, they generally like to give it to some sort of structured nonprofit organization, whether it's the Sierra Club or their local church. That way, they not only feel secure about where their money is going, but they know that they can write it off on *their* taxes without worrying about getting a letter from the IRS.

"You should think about setting up a foundation if you're going to do this every year," she said. "That way, not only will there be some structure for people to donate to, but it'll probably make it easier for you to get donations. People will feel better about giving it to an actual organization, especially if they know you've been around for a while."

"But that means I have to run the organization, like it's another business or something," I wailed, feeling a little bit overwhelmed. I didn't know much about nonprofits, but I had this vision in my mind of all these serious people in suits holding long serious meetings.

"Well, why don't we go talk to an attorney about setting up a nonprofit foundation?" she said. "It may not be as bad as it sounds."

So that's how the Oral Lee Brown Foundation was born. I knew quite a few attorneys through my work in real estate, so I called a few of them and asked if they knew anyone who specialized in creating new organizations. A number of people recommended a man named Fred Harvey, who's since become my attorney for everything related to the foundation. Mr. Harvey's the one who set up the Oral Lee Brown Foundation as a nonprofit, and he's kept us on track for everything we needed to do in order to retain that status. And Julie was right—it wasn't as complicated as I feared it would be. I had to develop a working board and have quarterly meetings, which I did. The original board members were myself, school principal Mrs. Peeks, and the Reverend Frank Gilbert. But those meetings didn't take too much time—the main purpose of the organization was to raise money.

That's really where the hard work came in, especially in the beginning. No one knew who we were or what we were trying to do, and we certainly didn't know what we were doing. It's no easy thing to be faced with this question every year: "How am I going to raise $10,000 from other people?" I knew that *I* could come up with $10,000 of my own money, and that if other people would do the same thing there wouldn't be any poor children struggling through this world without a proper education. But like I said, I knew that if you give people a service, they would be willing to pay for it, so for about a year the kids and I tried everything we could think of.

We could only offer the kinds of services that we were qualified to provide, and that meant car washes and bake sales and cook-outs. Pretty much everything we tried was, without a doubt, a disaster. It's lots of work to hold a bake sale or a barbecue. Some Saturdays the kids and I would work all day preparing the food and standing out on the block with signs. I probably wore through every tin in my kitchen baking cakes and pies for those bake sales, not to mention the cost of hot water and electricity it took to cook them and wash the dishes.

And then you know what? After we'd spent all that time and effort, I'd add up our proceeds for the day and we wouldn't clear $300. The barbecues were about the same, and they would even be worse because we'd have to spend the whole evening cleaning up after people. We only held one car wash because I knew immediately that that plan just wasn't going to work. The kids got wet, some got colds . . . and of course, the money just wasn't coming.

We tried a few other things, too. One of the kids had the idea for a raffle, so with lots of time and effort I talked an electronics store into donating a big-screen television. We spent a few weeks selling raffle tickets before we held the drawing. That was kind of fun, but like the bake sales and car washes, the money we raised was peanuts. A couple of hundred dollars—*maybe.* I realized pretty quickly that unless I was willing and able to devote every waking moment that I wasn't already spending either at work or with the kids, neighborhood fundraising wasn't going to make us our $10,000 in matching contributions. We would have to think bigger.

So at some point in 1988 I sat down and really got to thinking about what we could do to raise a lot of money at once. And the first thing that popped into my head was the idea of having a banquet. I remembered hearing ads on the radio about fancy charities putting on banquets where people would pay $1,000 a plate to have dinner and hear a speech from the president of the United States. I knew we couldn't get the president to speak at our banquet, but I thought that we could certainly get someone for whom people would be willing to pay, say, $50 a ticket. If we sold tickets for $50, I calculated, we could clear our $10,000 hurdle with just 200 tickets. That didn't factor in overhead costs, but I knew we could keep those low by getting donations, too.

With the annual banquet, we finally found something that worked. We raised $11,000 that first year, and to this day, the Oral Lee Brown Foundation has an annual banquet in Oakland. It's usually sometime in the fall, and of course now it's a much bigger affair than it was when we started. That first year we didn't have a clue what we were doing. In fact, I'd say that we didn't really know what we were doing until after a few years of trying. We made all the mistakes you can imagine: overbooking and underbooking venues, getting positive responses from two speakers and having to turn one of them away, hiring high-maintenance live bands and musicians.

Now that I've got a little bit more support around me from my foundation board and the people in the community, I've been able to find volunteers with experience in hosting banquets. We've been particularly successful applying for grants from large companies: Shell Oil Company and Wells Fargo Bank have supported us every year for the last five years and have really proved that the foundation is making a difference in children's lives. When you've had a bit of success, people are more confident about giving you their money.

It's still not easy for us, though. The foundation's been around for sixteen years and fund-raising is still difficult. Part of the problem is that asking people for money is something that I'm just not comfortable doing. I was always raised to take care of myself and make sure that I had the ability to provide for my own needs. With fund-raising you have to prove to people that your cause is something worth their money and their attention. It's difficult for me to try and prove that to people with patience, because I can't see anything more important than what we're doing!

When you ask people for money, you have to deal with a lot of negativity, and that's not easy either. When we first started holding annual banquets, I was amazed by how many people told me that they couldn't afford to buy a ticket because they had to send their own kids to school. I have to admit that I used to get a little bit of an attitude with people who said that. As I used to tell them, "These aren't my kids, either. And they still need to go to school. And if you're working like I am, and I can give them $10,000, you can certainly buy a $50 ticket."

But over the years I've learned to be more sympathetic to such arguments, and I think it's because of an experience I had with one woman, who shall remain nameless. It was without a doubt the most hurtful experience I've ever had as relates to these kids, but it taught me something. I asked her to buy a ticket for our annual banquet. She offered me a negative response with the excuse that she had her own kids to look after. I told her that these weren't my kids—that I had adopted them, was giving every cent that I could afford, and they needed to go to school. I needed help from the community to send them to school. "Now," I said to her, "I know you're part of the community. And I know you can afford a $50 ticket."

"All of that may be true," she said. "But you know what? I didn't adopt those kids. You did."

That hurt my feelings so much. I really believe that there are some things you should just keep to yourself if you can't say them in a nice way. She could've just kept telling me no, or even lied and claimed that she didn't have the money. But I respect her for telling the truth, because that *is* the truth. Nobody else adopted those kids but me. And no one else should have to pay for them if they don't want to. So if the buck stops right here at Oral Lee Brown's desk, I can't get angry at anyone for refusing to buy a ticket to our annual banquet, or refusing to give support in any other fashion. All I can do is thank them for their time and move on.

Ultimately, what really mattered to me in the end was doing all that I could do for these kids. It shocks people when I say this, but I can honestly say that I would've been all right if I had failed to put these kids through school. It would've been okay. Because I can't change the world all on my own. I can't make our banquets successful. I can't force anyone to buy a ticket. I couldn't have even made these kids go to college if they didn't want to go—and in fact, four of them didn't. But is that my failure? I don't think so. All I can do is the best that I can do with the tools that God has given me.

So if something had happened to stop us—say if I had lost my job—I would've been able to stand up in front of the media, including that reporter from Channel 5, in 1999. And I would've said, "I wasn't able to do it. In 1991, I lost my job and I couldn't spare $10,000 a year. I could only give $2,000 a year. But you know what? There are twenty-three kids here who have graduated from high school. Nineteen of them want to go to college. So if there's anyone here who's willing to step up and help them out, we'd love to hear from them right now."

And regardless of whether or not anyone stepped up to the plate and took my offer, I would've walked home and gone to sleep, and slept all night long. I wouldn't have been haunted in my dreams. Because I know that God would've been satisfied that I had done all that I could have.

Would it have bothered me if I failed to raise enough money? Oh, it would have bothered me to no end. It still bothers me today that four of my original babies chose not to go on to college. But failure was always a possibility that I was staring in the face. Anything could've happened—the bottom could've dropped out of the real estate market, or I could've been disabled, or all of the kids could've decided one day that they didn't want to go to college after all. When you're looking at the possibility of failures like that, you have to find a way to cope.

The way I learned to cope was to ask myself every evening,

Oral Brown, did you do everything that you could do for these kids today? I didn't ask if they were successful in doing everything they could for themselves, and I didn't ask if the rest of the world was successful in doing what they were supposed to do. I asked if *I* was successful in doing what I was supposed to do. And as long as the answer was yes, I put those worries to sleep for the night. Because 1999 was coming, the year my babies would graduate, and all I knew was that somehow, I had to keep going until then.

3

Meet the Class

Whenever I had to face cynical people, or negativity about what I was trying to do, I just thought about the kids I was fighting for. My babies are all very different—and they're all very special.

I had twenty-three in my first class alone, and at the moment I'm taking care of sixty students, so they can't all get a chapter in this book, but I'd like to draw you a picture of my first class of babies, so you can understand the difficulties they were facing when they came into their classrooms every morning. I'd say about two-thirds of my kids came from families where the primary breadwinner—and yes, it was usually their mother—was unemployed and on welfare. Two-thirds. And it's no coincidence that about two-thirds of my kids also came to school without eating breakfast first. That same number of kids would go home at night not knowing if they were having any dinner or, if they were having dinner, it might just be a sandwich or some instant noodles.

That may sound like a small, insignificant thing, but as I

learned, those sorts of small deprivations pointed to larger deprivations they were facing, too. Only one of these kids' parents had been to college, so it was obvious to me that we were going to have to struggle against a grinding cycle of poverty. Fortunately, these bright kids were more than prepared for anything. I'll just talk a little bit about each of them, so you can understand why they've come to mean so much to me.

The father of the class is definitely Jeffery Toney, who we'll get back to shortly. And if Jeffery's the father of the class, the mother of the class is Susan Richards, who wound up attending Merritt College right here in Oakland. Even as a little girl, Susan always knew what everyone was doing. She made it her business to keep everyone in line. During the weekend tutoring sessions that I started holding when the kids were in junior high school, Susan would be the one telling other kids, "You better stop fooling around and get to work on your math. And don't act like you can't do it, because I know you can."

She was often saying that to Tracy Easterling, who without a doubt embodied the indomitable spirit of this class. Like a lot of my babies, Tracy had a tough family life. Her parents were in and out of her life, so she depended on her grandmother for most of her childhood. That's a big part of the reason why she struggled to focus on her schoolwork, even though she was one of the brightest students in my class. I spent many an hour talking to Tracy about how she needed to get her grades up, because I knew that she could do better than she was doing — and she would do so, just to prove that I was right. She was attending college right here in Oakland when we lost her a couple of years ago. She was killed in a drive-by shooting that had absolutely nothing to do with her. Her death nearly tore my babies apart, and me too. Her spirit—and her pretty smile—lives with all of us now.

Delisha Cotton's another special girl. She's no bigger than a minute, but she's been taking care of herself and her little sister since she was fourteen. She did all the cooking, all the cleaning, everything. Her father was in the house, but Delisha did it all. And now she's gotten her undergraduate degree from UC Davis and is thinking about graduate school. But she's still just as sweet and down-to-earth as she can be.

Nekita Noel, who we'll also get back to, will probably be a judge for the state of California. She's had a serious interest in the law since she was in junior high school and I'm convinced that she'll go all the way to the top if that's what she wants. Another one of my kids with big dreams is LeAndre Miller. He's determined to play in the NBA. While I don't encourage any of my kids to depend on a career in sports for their future, I've seen this boy play. He's on the team at his school, Delta College in Stockton, California. And I may not be a basketball coach, but if anyone's got what it takes to play in the NBA, it's LeAndre.

Michael Tatmon loves basketball, too. He plays for his college team, California State University at Hayward. Michael's very bright—he's holding down a 3.26 grade point average, so he'll have the grades and the education to be successful at whatever he chooses to do with his life, even if he doesn't make it to the NBA.

But before you start thinking that all the boys want to play basketball, let me tell you about Curtis Richardson. From the time he was in grade school, he told me, "Miss Brown, I know the other kids want to be president, but I just want to be the greatest chef in the world." And I remember being surprised that a kid would want something like that, so I asked him, "But why don't you want to be president, too, Curtis?" And he just shook his head and went on. "The best chef in the world," he said. "That's what I'm going to do." He's currently studying at Laney College's culinary school, which I think is a pretty good start.

Another one with goals is Taisha Womack. She was a great kid—bright, happy, never gave me any trouble. She went to Contra Costa College in Contra Costa and decided that she wanted to be a nurse, so now she's thinking about going to Spelman next year for her graduate work. She came to me and we sat down and talked about it, and I told her the same thing I've told all the kids. "Whatever your goals are, whatever decisions you make about what you want to do with your life, I'll support you. You all are grown now and I'm here to listen to the choices you've made. If you decide to go on to graduate school, the foundation will find a way to pay for it."

We've got a couple of potential nurses in my class, actually—Krystal Cunningham, who was another one of my good, quiet students who always did her work and never got in any trouble, is currently studying nursing at Howard University in Washington, D.C. One of her friends at Howard is Kela Paris, who's also one of my babies. Both of these girls—along with Jorge Carapia, who's studying business at the University of California at Berkeley—were *exactly* the kinds of kids that people *don't* think of when they think about children who go to school in the ghetto: smart, diligent, hardworking kids who are making their way in the world despite the odds.

I'll admit that I did get upset with some of my kids who decided not to go to college at all. I sometimes have to remind myself that they all have different circumstances in their lives that might make it difficult for them to get to school at this particular moment. Like Teisha Beverly, who wanted to be a marine biologist. She was accepted at San Diego State and really wanted to go, but at the last moment she had to turn down the invitation in order to stay home and take care of her mother. I was disappointed, but that shows the generosity of Teisha's spirit. She always loved her family first, and most. That's a beautiful thing, and I can't believe that God isn't watching that kind of behavior. I sure am, and despite her decision, I know that Teisha will go on to make an important contribution to the world.

Erica Lincoln's another one that I'm watching carefully. She was an A student from the time she was in grade school. She's not in school right now, even though she graduated from an honors program at her high school. "I just need a break, Mrs. Brown," she said. Well, okay, Erica. It's tough for some of these kids, especially the sensitive ones who've been raised in difficult environments. I'm not going to judge any of them about what they've chosen to do. But I let Erica know that I'm expecting great things out of her, because I know that she has everything she needs to do whatever she wants. "I know, Mrs. Brown!" she said. "And I'll get there. It may take me a little bit longer than everyone else, but I'll get there." I can understand that sentiment—I've lived my life the same way.

Another one who's still recovering from a very difficult time is Joseph Scurlock. Joseph's father raised him. Without getting too much into his personal business, I think that it was hard for Joseph to grow up without his mother. He's such a sensitive child. He's been trying to figure out his personal relationships ever since. But he's a bright kid—he went to the University of Nevada at Las Vegas. And even though he didn't finish college, he is slowly finding his way, and I'm certain that he will find another route toward a positive and successful adulthood.

Tamara Walton impressed me when she was a child because she was always reading. I never saw her without a book in her hand. For a long time she wanted to be a doctor, I believe because she had an aunt in Atlanta who was a doctor and they were very close all throughout high school. Role models are so important to these kids, and even though I've done the best I can, I know that I can't provide them with all the support they'll need. And even when I try, some of my kids just surprise me—like LaQuita and LaQuonda White, for example.

Quita and Quonda, as we call them, are sisters. They're less than a year apart, Quonda being the elder, and they were in the same first-grade class at Brookfield. I scratch my head about these two girls, because they grew up in the same home, had the same mother and father, and pretty much everything one experienced the other experienced also. And yet they turned out to be two very different people: Quita is doing very well for herself at San Jose State, while Quonda went to a junior college for one semester and then decided not to continue. They're both sweet girls, but one of them wanted to continue her education and the other didn't. This isn't to say that Quonda won't choose to do so one day, but it goes to show that all I can do is offer these kids love and support, but, like any parent I don't have the final say-so in what they do as adults.

Speaking of kids with unexpected behavior, Winter Woods is a prime example. Due to her family situation, she was placed in the care of the state and later adopted by the Woods family. That would be enough to traumatize any kid, but Winter was always the sweetest girl. Wherever we went as a class, she always wanted to sit on my lap or lie in my arms. You'd think that she'd have a lot of anger toward the world or find it hard to trust people, considering what she'd been through, but it was just the opposite. She always found some goodness in people.

If you want to talk about surprises, though, let's talk about Robert Porter. He was certainly not one of the best students at Brookfield, or when he got to high school. Instead he was a serious young man who always concentrated on his family first. But once he got the chance to go to college — he went to Southern Baton Rouge University — he blossomed, holding down a 3.84 grade point average. It just goes to show that you can't make assumptions about how a person's going to turn out.

For example, lots of people liked to make assumptions about my baby Robin Travis. Robin had a baby when she was sixteen years old. Now, that's every parent's worst nightmare, isn't it? But Robin took care of that baby better than anyone could have imagined, and she did it with no help at all. She didn't complain, didn't fall behind, just did what she needed to do to take care of her child and kept on stepping. She graduated from high school just a little bit late and she's now studying at American River College in Sacramento. And her baby girl is six years old and about to go to first grade herself.

I'm guilty of making assumptions, too. I'll be the first one to admit that of all my kids, Cory Edwards was the last one that I would've thought would ever make anything of his life. I was particularly disappointed when he called me up in his second year of college and told me that he wanted to leave. In fact, I was more than disappointed—I was angry. I'd already spent $32,000 on this boy's college education and now he was telling me that he didn't want to stay?

"Cory," I said, "I sent you there and I'll bring you back. Let me know when you're ready and I'll send you a plane ticket."

So he came back to Oakland. And he hadn't been back in town for more than two weeks when a house on 98th Avenue caught on fire. It looked like the whole block might go up in flames. Cory, who happened to be walking down the street, ran right into the blaze and came back out with a grandmother and a little child who weren't able to get out in time. He saved their lives—all by himself!

The entire fire department gave him special recognition that day. But even better, one of the firemen was so impressed that he took Cory under his wing and offered to teach him what he needed to know to be a fireman. He's expected to be a full-fledged fireman with the Solano County Fire Department as early as next year. And he will be a successful man, I know it. He just had to find his own way to get there. The fact that he did so makes me proud.

Finally, there's LaTosha Hunter. She's always been the star of the class, and you mark my words, the world will know her one day. She graduated from Alcorn State University in Mississippi last year, dean's list every semester. Right now she's studying for her master's degree in accounting at Jackson State University. And I love all my babies more than life itself, but if I could be anyone else in the world, I would want to be LaTosha Hunter. She's just that good. When you meet LaTosha, you can tell immediately that she will be well known throughout the country, or even the world if she wants to be. She's got that kind of talent and the ambition to match. But the thing I like most about LaTosha is that she remains aware of where she came from and what she needs to do about it. For example, she could have worked in lots of high-flying accounting firms the summer after her first year of graduate school. But she chose to work at an excellent firm in Oakland, in part so she could be around to help out at the foundation.

And those are my babies. And just to give you a better idea of who they are and where they came from, I'm going to talk a little bit more about two of them: Jeffery Toney and Nekita Noel.

⚶

Both Jeffery and Nekita grew up in the neighborhood around Brookfield Elementary School. Most people who lived in Brookfield, as it's known, were low income, and most of them were African-American. Probably over half of the community was made up of single-parent families. If you ran across a two-parent household, chances were good that it was two grandparents raising their grandkids. The grandparents were also usually a bit better off than the parents in Brookfield, because they had pensions and fixed incomes that paid more than a minimum-wage job.

Speaking of minimum-wage jobs, there weren't many places to get them in Brookfield. When my kids were in elementary school, the neighborhood didn't have a grocery store or the sorts of retail stores that provide employment to lower-income neighborhoods. There were no shopping centers. Brookfield didn't even have a bank. It had check-cashing stores, liquor stores, and a couple of tiny corner groceries that charged twice what you'd pay in a regular supermarket.

So that's the environment we're talking about. And into this environment comes my baby Jeffery Toney. He's got one younger brother and three older sisters, but he grew up with just one of his sisters and his mother. His father was around sometimes, but they're not really close—in fact, Jeffery isn't close to any of his family members at all. "I'm closer to Mrs. Brown than I am to any of my family," I overheard Jeffery saying once. It shocked me, but maybe if you hear the rest of his history you'll understand.

Jeffery's family moved around a lot. Often his mother couldn't keep up with the rent or struggled to make payments on their house. So when they fell behind, they had to move. Jeffery went to five different elementary schools in Oakland.

In case you're wondering, yes, that means Jeffery wasn't at Brookfield with the rest of the kids for their elementary school years. He left after the first grade, simply disappeared—no one knew where to find him or how to get in touch with him. After a few years I had given up all hope of contacting him. I believed that just like the little girl at Hub Liquor Store who inspired this whole program, I'd never find him.

"But I never forgot you, Mrs. Brown," he told me once about those years. "I remember you because you gave me a present for Christmas that first-grade year. I didn't get many presents for Christmas, so I was excited before I even saw it. And then you gave it to me and guess what it was? A leather wallet. Who else but you would give a six-year-old a leather wallet for Christmas? I felt so grown up."

Jeffery felt really grown up because of that present, but of course, he was just a kid. He had to go where his mother went, so he spent his years in elementary school moving around and around, always being the new kid in school. He went to E. Morris Cox, Whittier, and Burbank Elementary Schools. He and his family stayed on 55th, 60th, 62nd, 64th, 98th, and Courtland Avenues. They also lived in motels up and down MacArthur Boulevard. He mostly stayed with his mother during this time, although sometimes he would visit his father.

"But I never lived with my father," Jeffery said. "And life with my mom meant I was never staying in the same place for long."

Even with all that disruption, he still managed to shine as something special. I was very happy to learn later on that Jeffery had a teacher at Burbank Elementary, Mr. Brooks, who provided him with real concern and encouragement. Mr. Brooks was his fifth-grade teacher. He hired Jeffery to clean up his yard so that Jeffery could get a feeling for how hard you have to work to earn money legitimately. He also got Jeffery involved with a Big Brother program he had started, so that Jeffery would have access to lots of positive male role models. And he urged Jeffery to stay focused on his studies.

"He sort of played the role that Mrs. Brown played in my life later on," Jeffery said. "I mean literally, from the field trips on down. He helped me out and recognized that I was more than just another kid in the neighborhood, running around and stealing bikes."

But by the time he met Mr. Brooks, Jeffery had already

grown used to tough times. His mother, who he loves tremendously, was not able to take care of him financially the way we all hope a mother can. And so, like many low-income kids, Jeffery started fending for himself at an early age.

It helped that he had a naturally positive attitude and a sense of direction. Jeffery may not know exactly where he's going, and he may not have any shoes on his feet to get there, but you can believe that he'll find a way. Even in the first grade he once got my attention by pulling on the bottom of my jacket. I turned to him, and all I saw was that little stuck-out lip and a fierce expression.

"What is going on with you, Jeffery?" I asked.

"Mrs. Brown," he said importantly.

"What, Jeffery?"

"Mrs. Brown, one day I'm going to be something."

"Yeah, you're something today, Jeffery."

"No, Mrs. Brown, one day I'm *really* going to be something."

"Okay, Jeffery. Why don't you go back to your seat now?"

Six years old! He had absolutely no reason to believe that this world would let him become anything, especially since he didn't even have a chance to stay in one place long enough to catch his breath. But even at that age Jeffery was a natural leader. I remember watching him on the playground during the first grade. All of my babies could be wild and willful, and sometimes I couldn't even get them all together to play a game. But Jeffery could. He'd have everyone lined up in two minutes, ready to listen to whatever he had to say.

So you can imagine that I missed him for the next seven years that he was separated from the program. In my mind, he had never really left the program, and even if I hadn't seen him again until the day of his high school graduation, the foundation still would have paid for him to go to college. A promise is a promise. And as it happened, he did find his way back to us. It was sheer luck. In the ninth grade, he happened to go to Castlemont High School, which is the same school to which most of my babies went. One day, when he was on the school bus, he met Tracy Easterling.

"I just remember being on the bus and hearing this girl who was so loud," Jeffery said. "There was no way I could've missed her—there was no way any of us could've missed her. And then she started staring at me."

Somehow, Tracy recognized him. She ran up to Jeffery and gave him a big hug, shouting, "You were in the program with us, Mrs. Brown's gonna pay for you to go to college!"

"I didn't know *what* she was talking about," Jeffery said. "I hadn't heard anything about no college, and I definitely hadn't heard about someone paying for it."

Tracy kept talking, and by the time they got off the bus Jeffery was curious enough to follow her to my office on East 14th Street. I recognized him as soon as he walked in—I was floored, but I knew him immediately.

"I've been looking for you," was all that I could say. He looked confused, and I stammered on about how he was still part of the program; how I had never given up on him—he must have thought I was crazy, but I didn't care. I felt like I was welcoming home a long-lost son—and I suppose I was.

Jeffery decided to rejoin the program, affirming my belief that he was a super-special kid. You see, my other babies were with me all the way through. I had seven extra years, seven *formative* years, to drill into them my message about college and education. I suppose you could say I didn't give them much of a choice to disagree with me. But Jeffery hadn't gotten all that, and in fact his whole childhood had been so unstable that I'm surprised he agreed to get off the bus with Tracy at all. Her promise about college must have sounded like he had just won the sweepstakes—why would Jeffery have believed her? Especially since his chief experience with people regarding promises was that they were always broken.

But he did believe Tracy, and that just goes to show that Jeffery has always wanted something more than what he saw in his environment. He fell right back in with the group. Most of them remembered him vaguely or remembered seeing him at one or another neighborhood event. Those who didn't, took to him quickly and warmly.

"When we came together it was like family," Jeffery said. "We've all experienced tough things, and even if we couldn't exactly relate to someone's specific problem, we knew what caused it—just the condition of not having enough."

Jeffery ran into that condition headlong during high school. When he first found us again in the ninth grade, he wanted two things: he wanted to be an engineer, and he wanted to go to Morehouse College in Atlanta. Morehouse is one of the best-known historically black colleges, and it may be second only to Spelman in terms of national regard. I remember Jeffery's reaction to Morehouse when we went on the college tour a couple years later; he looked like he was coming home.

"That was a wonderful tour," Jeffery said. "It was my first time on an airplane, my first time really leaving home . . . it just felt good. And I really wanted to go to Morehouse, but reality set in when I got back."

Reality was Jeffery and math. The struggles he experienced with algebra and geometry in the ninth and tenth grades led him to think that maybe engineering, which is so focused on math, wasn't for him. So he started to concentrate on what he could do well, namely performing. Jeffery is a wonderful singer. Maybe one day you'll be able to hear him sing at one of our annual banquets. He even wrote a song about me, calling me his angel!

In tenth grade Jeffery got a record deal with a small label, and increasingly he shifted his focus toward the music world. Ordinarily that would have made me nervous, because the music world is second only to the NBA in terms of disappointing poor young black kids with big dreams. But Jeffery, always practical, envisions a career for himself that includes business entrepreneurship.

"Working for someone else isn't where it's at," Jeffery said. "If you own everything that you create, you don't have to split your profits with someone else who didn't put their heart and soul into it. And black people have lost too much already by letting other people own their music."

But just as Jeffery was building his dreams for the future about the music business, his life in the present started to fall apart. When he was sixteen years old, his mother fell on hard financial times. They fell behind on rent and were evicted from their house, and Jeffery didn't want to go where his mother and her boyfriend were moving. At first he stayed with a family friend, but after a few months she had to let him go, and Jeffery was officially homeless.

"At this point my entire life took a shift," Jeffery said. "Everything that I'd been working for—college, my music, all of it—had to be pushed to the back burner. I had to worry about eating and surviving."

He spoke to one of his cousins, Fatimah, who owns a small hair salon in Oakland. She agreed to let him stay in her shop, the World's Best Braids, at night in exchange for a weekly fee. (When Jeffery left for college, she gave Jeffery all the money that he had given her in rent. "To get me started in Chicago. Which was great because otherwise I would've had nothing when I got there," Jeffery said.) He slept on the floor in the braid shop for a long time. Some nights he would spend the night at a friend's house or even in his car.

As for eating, Jeffery hustled. "I was out in the streets, doing bad things," Jeffery said. "Was I happy about that? Absolutely not. On the other hand, I'd be even unhappier if I didn't, because then I wouldn't have had anything to eat."

He kept quiet at our foundation meetings about what his life was like during those days. I remember asking Jeffery if things were okay, if he needed money or anything. "I'm cool, Mrs. Brown, I don't need anything," he would tell me. I think some of it has to do with pride, and with a certain idea of manhood. Like lots of young men, Jeffery didn't like it when a woman offered to give him money—even me. Sometimes I would just have to tell him, "You know what, Jeff, I don't want to hear it. Take this money and go do what you need to do. When you get grown and start making your own paycheck, if you still want to pay me back, you can pay me back then." But it was difficult for Jeffery to take money from me, because he felt that as a man—even though he wasn't grown yet—he should be able to take care of himself.

Jeffery was homeless during his junior and senior years of high school, which are the crucial years as far as college applications are concerned. The men and women who sit on application decision boards really focus on those last two years, especially the junior year. And I'd venture to guess that most juniors in high school who are thinking about the college application process don't have to endure what Jeffery did, which is one reason why I get upset when college administrators talk about how they can't find nearly enough "qualified" students from low-income backgrounds. How many high school juniors could take care of themselves like Jeffery did? And the incredible thing is that Jeffery always got his homework done, no matter what kind of situation he was in. His high school grade point average never fell below a 3.0.

"It's funny, because college really slipped off my radar screen during those years," Jeffery said. "But I still made sure I did everything I needed to do to keep up with my academics—I always got my work done, even if I had to do it in my car while I was hustling, and I still went to the foundation's tutoring sessions."

And once again, it was a special teacher who got Jeffery back on track.

"Her name was Miss Leah Oliver," Jeffery said. "And I have to say, one of the reasons why I listened to her is that she was cute. I had a crush on her."

Miss Oliver was a learning disabilities teacher at Castlemont. Jeffery was not in her class, but she took him under her wing. Realizing that the school's overburdened guidance counselors might let Jeffery slip through the cracks, she took over the role that they should have been playing. During his senior year, she bugged him about his grades and reminded him about deadlines for college applications.

"It's a good thing that she did," Jeffery said. "Because I was procrastinating. I may not have applied to college at all if she hadn't sent for the college brochures."

Miss Oliver is originally from Chicago. Recognizing Jeffery's ambitions, she suggested that he go to a school in her hometown—Columbia College, a small school that focuses on the music business. She called Columbia and asked them to send her some information and an application, then called Jeffery into her office.

"As soon as I looked at the school's mission and read some of the course descriptions, I knew it was exactly what I was looking for," Jeffery said. "It was different from a regular music school, because there were business classes mixed in with the creative side of things. Columbia really focused on getting students ready for the music *business*, not just preparing them to be *musicians*."

Jeffery didn't need any more prompting. He applied to Columbia—it was the only school he applied to—and was accepted. I was ecstatic that Jeffery would be going to college and getting out of Oakland for a little while. A change of scenery would do him good, I thought, and besides it would be nice for him to be in a stable environment. Sure enough, Jeffery blossomed at Columbia.

"The fact that I was on my own so much during high school really helped me to prepare for the stresses of college," Jeffery said. "I didn't have any trouble with homesickness or time management like a lot of the other students. The only thing that was difficult for me to adapt to was the weather."

Once at Columbia, Jeffery got interested in other facets of the music business, like production. One year, he asked if I would give him a new computer for Christmas rather than buying him a plane ticket home. He spent his Christmas break on that computer, teaching himself how to use it, and now he's a whiz with production programs and graphics. In fact, I occasionally ask him to help me with the graphics for foundation materials.

Now Jeffery is studying at the University of California–Los Angeles, getting a music business certificate and preparing himself to go back to school for an MBA. He's told me that he wants to be the next Russell Simmons, and I see absolutely no reason why he can't be. But who would've thought that he'd eventually end up at UCLA after hustling in the streets at age sixteen?

"There are a lot of Jefferys out there, and they're standing at a crossroads just like I was when I was sixteen," Jeffery said. "They're bright, they're willing to work hard, but unless they've got good role models who are willing to put in some time with them, most of them just won't see a different way of surviving other than what they've learned on the streets. If I hadn't had the role models I had, like Mr. Brooks and Mrs. Brown and Miss Oliver, I wouldn't have seen a way out. As it was, it would've been very easy for me to take the other road."

And that's why I'm continuing the foundation's work by finding new students, because like he says, there are a lot of Jefferys out there. And I know how fortunate I am that none of my original babies took that other road. Because every single one of them had the temptation to do so at some point.

❧

Nekita Noel knows how easy it is for poor young kids to fall into hustling, which is one reason why she wants to spend her life helping the ones who have already fallen. She's just finished her undergraduate studies in criminal justice and is now doing graduate work at the California State University at Hayward. She's studying criminal justice and social work, and she's even thinking about going to law school *after* she gets her master's degree.

"I want to keep all my options open as far as working with young people in the justice system," she said. "I think I can be a real inspiration to them."

She's certainly a real inspiration to me. Nekita was born in San Diego, and her family moved to East Oakland when she was a baby. Her father is a merchant seaman, so the family moved around quite a bit before her parents got divorced. She was part of the original first-grade class at Brookfield, but she left in the second grade when her family moved to Louisiana. Nekita was in Louisiana for second grade and part of third grade. Then her family moved back to Oakland, to a small house on 96th Avenue and Sunnyside. That's a different school district than Brookfield, so Nekita finished elementary school at E. Morris Cox.

"Because we moved around so much while I was in elementary school, I didn't really get to know Mrs. Brown until middle school and even high school," Nekita said. "I certainly didn't understand the program fully until I was in the ninth grade."

Fortunately, Nekita was already determined to go to college by then.

"During the fifth grade, I went on a school trip to Stanford," Nekita said. "And as soon as I set foot on that campus, I knew that I needed to go to college. It's something I've known I was going to do ever since then. It was just a matter of getting there."

She knew, too, that she wanted to work with young people who have gotten tangled up in the criminal justice system. Some of that came from living in East Oakland, where so many of our young people are introduced to the harshness of the system early.

"I've lived in East Oakland for most of my life," Nekita said. "When I was growing up there, I didn't see it as a good area or a bad area—it was just home. But as I got older I started to realize that there were things going on there that I didn't see in other parts of Oakland, especially as far as violence goes. That got me wondering if there were things we could do about it."

Nekita thought that one of the problems in East Oakland had to do with the fact that so many of our young people there are exposed to the criminal justice system at such a young age. Most of them aren't committing crimes at the age of ten, but maybe they're watching their parents or older siblings be hauled off to jail by the police. Or maybe they're being removed from their homes at that age and placed in foster care. Those kinds of disruptions can harden kids at an early age and make it easier for them to make the transition to crime themselves. *Unless someone steps in,* Nekita thought.

"I think if I can catch these young kids before they start getting into crime, or at least before they start getting into *serious* crime, I can let them know that there's more to life than what they've seen," Nekita said.

Even in high school she started reaching out to younger people, trying to get them to see that they didn't have to repeat the cycle. She lectured her younger cousins about finding a way out of poverty. Plus, Nekita has five nieces and nephews to practice on.

"I'm still talking to them about it all the time, even though my nieces and nephews are too young to really know what I'm talking about," Nekita said. "You know, when I pick them up from preschool, I say, I saw you chasing that boy on the playground. Don't you know there's more to life than chasing boys? Don't you know there's more to it than being somebody's mama? And they just roll their eyes at me. But at least they're starting to hear that message early."

After she finishes her graduate work, Nekita plans to start her own program for young people. She wants to work with young people who are either in the criminal justice system or at risk of falling into it. Her plan is to offer them mentoring and training programs.

"Mrs. Brown's program with us has really been the model for what I want to do," said Nekita. "I'm not necessarily going to tell all the kids in my program that they should go to college, because that's not for everyone. Some people might want to take up a trade, or start a small business, and I think that's great. But I want them to see that there are options for getting out of the ghetto, just like Mrs. Brown showed us."

That's her goal, and she'll be the first to tell you that she knows it won't be easy. To start this kind of a program, she'll need expertise in criminal justice, law, and social work.

"I might be in school for a long time," Nekita said.

Fortunately, Nekita thrives under a challenge. She had a big challenge adjusting to her first college, the California State University at Chico. The academics at Castlemont High School didn't prepare her for the work she was expected to do at college.

"I thought I was the biggest idiot," Nekita said. "I didn't know what a thesis was. I didn't know how to focus my papers on one subject; I didn't even know how to *type*. I really started to see the difference between kids who had gone to schools in good neighborhoods and the kids like me, who went to schools like Castlemont. I spent a lot of time playing catch-up."

The biggest adjustment, however, was a social one. Chico is a rural community centered around the college. Nekita was used to being in an urban environment. As for her classmates, the college is well known as a party school for fraternity and sorority types. Nekita is neither a party girl nor a sorority type. She also had to deal with a racist landlady who called me every other day to report on what she thought Nekita was doing wrong.

"Let's just say that I loved the school but not the community," Nekita said.

Eventually she decided to transfer to California State University at Sacramento. Sacramento State is more diverse than Chico. The students are also a little bit more mature: many of them live off-campus or work their way through school, and Nekita found it easier to relate to them.

After she finished her bachelor's degree, Nekita started her graduate school classes at Hayward State. Right now she lives in Hayward with her family. She doesn't plan to live in East Oakland again.

"It's hard for me to go back there sometimes," Nekita said. "Lots of people I know have gotten killed. It's where I grew up, but it's not something I want to be a part of for the rest of my life."

But she still comes by the foundation to help out.

"I think Mrs. Brown is a brave woman to do what she did," Nekita said. "I don't know that I'd have done it."

Nekita actually told me that once, and I had to smile. "You'd have done *more*," is what I told her. "You *will* do more. You're going to help kids who have already gotten into trouble, and that's work that needs to be done, too."

"Well, let's just hope I can do as well as you've done, Mrs. Brown," she said.

4

The Elementary Years

All my babies are wonderful children who have grown up
to be incredible young men and women. None of them gave
me the trouble that some of their peers might have. That said,
when I started going to Brookfield Elementary School to
work with them, I still had to face the fact that I was going to
be responsible for a classroom of twenty-three energetic little kids. The teacher, Mrs. Waters, was there, too, because
she had laid down the law and was very firm with those kids,
so that they didn't run her out of the classroom! So before I
went into the classroom for that first time, I sat down and
steeled myself. "Okay, Oral Lee," I said. "You're going to have
to set some ground rules for these kids if you want to survive
this!"

So I raised these kids the same way I raised my own kids.
If I had to put my philosophy in a paragraph, it would go
something like this: "I'm grown and you are not. That's number one. I'm the Mama and you're a kid. So whatever I ask
you to do, I expect you to do it. If you don't, I will take appro-

priate steps to punish you. Now if by chance I find out that I was wrong, I will come and apologize. But if by chance you find out that I was wrong, you write it down, and when you're twenty-one years old you bring it to me and we can talk about it. Until then, I'm the adult here and you're the kid. And you're supposed to have a kid's place."

Maybe that's a harsh way to raise kids. I sure know that I hated it when my mama and daddy said things like that. I would pout for hours when they pulled out that argument to explain why I had to do this or that. But when I got older I realized that they were right. They were the ones paying the bills. They were the ones feeding me. I was just living there on their good graces, so it wasn't asking too much for me to do what they said. And by the time you're grown yourself, those things that you thought they did wrong when you were a kid don't matter anyway. Parents surely leave some mistakes for you to make on your own, and by that point you're learning your own lessons.

Now in the case of these kids, they weren't living in my house, but I was taking care of them all the same. I wasn't taking care of them in the way that their parents were, but then I really don't think the things I was asking them to do were unreasonable. I asked them to go to school. I asked them to do their homework. I asked them to obey their parents. And I asked them to think about what they could do to improve a bad situation before running to me with it. "I don't want to hear anything about your teacher likes everyone else in the classroom but doesn't like you," I told them. "It's okay if she doesn't like you. She's not there to like you. She's there to teach you. And if she doesn't like you, maybe there's something you can do to make that situation better. Like not acting up in class."

Granted, there are some times when a kid's protests against the teacher are totally valid. And there were many occasions throughout my time with these kids when I confronted their teachers myself, if I felt they weren't doing what they were supposed to do or that they were being unfair to my kids. But the way I see it, it wasn't for the kids to know when I was angry with their teachers. I thought it was better that the teachers and I presented a united front when it came to the purpose of educating these children. Besides, I thought it was a way for them to learn an important lesson about dealing with the unpleasant people and situations they would have to deal with throughout their lives: that even under difficult circumstances, they will be expected to, and should, do whatever job they are there to do.

"God didn't put you in this world for people to like you," I told them. "He put you here to contribute something. And by the same token, you're not in this classroom for the teacher to like you. You're here to learn. If your teacher doesn't like you, I don't want to hear it. Now if she's not teaching you, if you're not learning anything, then we have a problem. That's when you come to me."

I said the same sorts of things to their parents, when they would complain to me that they couldn't get their kids to do their homework. "Why don't you turn that TV off?" I suggested. And then they hemmed and hawed about how they needed to watch TV when they were cooking dinner or that they didn't want to be "mean" to their kids. "Why are you afraid of being mean?" I said to them. "Put your foot down.

Turn off that TV and tell your kids to come inside the house. And let them know that you're serious. If you're not mean with them now, somebody else, like the cops, is going to be mean with them later. Now what would you rather see?"

I get so angry when I hear excuses like these coming from parents. If you're a parent, you can't be your kid's best friend. You need to be a parent. Be stern. Demand the best out of your kids and let them know that you won't accept anything less. Sure, your kids are going to be upset, but they'll get over it. And later on they'll appreciate the fact that you were tough on them.

I believe that some of the parents took my advice, thank the Lord. If they hadn't, there was no way I would've been able to keep those kids in line while they were on my watch. I would tell them, "I didn't dream up the idea of making rules for kids. Someone told them to me. And all of us out here in Oakland now are scared to raise our kids, because the law and everyone else has told us it's not right to discipline them. Uh-uh. You better take that power back. And you better tell them while you're whupping them that you love them." Some of those adults would shake their heads at me and say, "Oh, no, Miss Brown, you're too mean."

Well, maybe so. But I've seen way too many kids, not more than sixteen or seventeen years old, out here getting their faces beaten to a pulp by the police, and all because no one ever taught them how to behave. Children need to learn discipline, whether it's in the classroom or with their peers. And sometimes you can discipline kids by talking to them, but when they're younger, sometimes you need to use a switch. I never hurt my kids or did anything that would've alarmed Social

Services. But I let them know that there were certain behaviors that I wouldn't accept when they were kids, and as a result they have become well-behaved adults.

Did all of their parents follow my advice? Surely not. Hey, I wasn't living in their house, so maybe it was a little presumptuous of me to tell them how to raise their kids. But I did get to know all of those parents very well over those years in elementary school, mostly through my own efforts. I wanted them to know who was spending all this time with their kids, so I made sure to introduce myself to each and every one. In most cases it was as simple as making phone calls to the parents every once in a while to see how things were going, and staying to talk to them after our monthly meetings at Brookfield. We started talking and getting to know about each other's lives.

Even though they were only in elementary school, my kids were no fools. They knew when something was going wrong at home, and they found ways to tell me. They never did it in an obvious way—poor kids understand better than anyone the shame of being poor, and they'll do everything they can to hide what's going on—but I really believed that I was one of their parents too. And any kind of parent is going to notice that something's wrong, that their kid is coming to school with holes in his shoes or an empty belly.

So I would ask Mrs. Waters about it, and she said to me, "I don't have the time to investigate, but I noticed that there's something wrong too. Why don't you take so-and-so aside and ask him what's going on?" So, starting in the first grade, I took those kids outside, and asked them, "Now, what's wrong? You've had your head hanging down all day. You couldn't get enough to eat at lunchtime, and you've been wearing these same pants to school for the last week."

The experience I had with my kids in elementary school showed me that if you show a kid that you love him and that you're concerned about him, this technique can actually work. My kids would almost always tell me what the problem was, even in those first few years of elementary school. They'd ask me not to tell their mother, then they'd pour out the problem — and it was usually related to the typical problems of poverty and deprivation that affect children in low-income families: Mama doesn't feed me in the morning, they'd say. Or Mama's working two jobs and can't ever be there when I get home from school, so some neighborhood bullies have been beating me up and taking my dinner money. Or none of us kids have gotten any new clothes in the last two years.

And that's how I found myself getting more and more involved in these kids' lives. What I originally set out as my adoption strategy—put away $10,000 a year, and visit the school a couple of times a week—quickly mushroomed into something far beyond anything I could have imagined. I knew I was getting myself into a big commitment, but I had no idea just *how* big. I didn't know I was going to be buying clothes and food and shoes. I *certainly* didn't know I was going to spend whatever spare time I did have taking these kids on field trips and picnics.

But by listening to these kids in school—and yes, by coming to love them—I realized that they couldn't actually learn if they didn't have the proper tools to do it with. By proper tools I mean first of all, breakfast, lunch, and dinner, along with clothes on their backs and shoes on their feet. Not to mention the chance to get out of the classroom every once in a while, to see how the things they were learning in books translated into the real world. Their parents worked as hard as they could to give them those tools, but most of them weren't able to do it all. I was there to pick up the slack. And it all started in elementary school, with me asking the kids a few simple questions.

I remember, for example, one day when the kids were still in first grade. Mrs. Waters was teaching a math lesson, and she asked me to take a few of the kids aside who were having trouble and go over the problems with them. I don't remember who exactly the kids were, but it seems to me that one of them was Robert Porter, who eventually went on to hold down a 3.84 GPA at Southern Baton Rouge University. We were going over the questions, and I just asked them innocently what else they were doing in class.

"All we do is sit here in this classroom," said Robert. "Mrs. Waters won't let us go anywhere."

"Well, where would you like to go?"

"Why can't we go to the playground and have a picnic? Or go somewhere other than school, like on a field trip or something?"

Well, the simple answer was that the school district didn't have any money for field trips, and that's why they couldn't go. Mrs. Waters, like most teachers in public schools, already spent far too much of her own money buying things for her classroom that should have been supplied by the school district, things like pencils and textbooks and posters. But hearing their comments made me think: Well, why couldn't they go? I didn't know much about school funding, but I could guess that the wealthy kids in the Oakland hills got to go on whatever field trips they wanted. I'm a big believer that kids learn as much outside of the classroom as they do inside of it, and if they wanted to do fun, educational things, then why shouldn't they? Of course, that also meant that I would have to take charge, because there was no one else to do it.

So that's how I started our program of extracurricular activities. During those elementary school years, the kids were small, so we mostly stayed close to home, but there was plenty to do even at that: the Monterey Bay Aquarium, Oakland A's baseball games, picnics, the Oakland Zoo . . . I tried to organize every outing I could think of, and I asked them for suggestions, too. For the most part, they just wanted to do regular things that kids enjoy doing, like having sleepovers, for instance. It's hard for most adults to believe, but my kids wouldn't have had sleepovers under normal circumstances. They lived in neighborhoods that were dangerous, with poor parental supervision. The notion of having a gaggle of kids over, with sleeping bags and popcorn and all the rest of it, wasn't as easy in East Oakland as it might have been somewhere else.

So I had sleepovers at my house. I could never have more than four kids at the same time, but throughout the year I'd have four girls over at my house, and then four boys. It went on that way until I'd had the whole class over. I drew up a permission slip for their parents to sign, claiming responsibility for the kids' safety while they were at my house. Their parents knew me, so they had no problem with trusting their kids to me for the night. And the kids had a great time at the sleepovers. We watched movies and had pillow fights, and in the morning I made pancakes for everyone. When I dropped them off at home, I always felt really good that they'd had the opportunity to have some relaxed, innocent fun—the kind of fun experiences of which every childhood should be full.

We also did lots of seasonal things. Around the holiday season, we made Christmas ornaments out of construction paper and wrote class cards to Mrs. Waters. The spring and early summer meant lots of barbecues. I made a special effort to have activities in the summer because that was a good way of keeping the kids in touch with one another.

None of these activities were expensive, and no extracurricular activities *have* to be expensive if you're willing to use your imagination. I explained my situation to the management of the Oakland A's, and they were nice enough to give us free tickets whenever we asked. Instead of buying the food at the concession stand I filled up my husband's big thermos with Kool-Aid and brought that, along with hot dogs that I'd grilled in my own oven the night before. When we went to the Oakland Zoo the charge was only $1 per car, so I got some of my friends to join us. We packed the kids into three cars and there you go: an outing for $3. For our very first outing, which was a picnic at the Brookfield Recreation Center, I bought the food out of my own pocket, but it was just hot dogs and baked beans and potato salad. It couldn't have cost more than $100, and the kids just had a ball.

Mrs. Waters would sometimes shake her finger at me about all these activities and say, "Now, Mrs. Brown, don't take on too much. You'll get burned out if you're not careful." And I would just laugh and say, "But I want to do it, Mrs. Waters, I really do." And I didn't just want to do it for my kids, either. Whenever we had extra food from the picnics, I'd invite the kids in other classes to come over and share it with us. And inevitably when I went to pick up my kids at their houses for our field trips on Saturdays, some of them would ask if they could bring their little brothers or sisters with us. Or their parents would say that I *had* to take all the kids so that they could go get something done. I love kids, so I'd just scoop them all up and find space for them somewhere in the car.

That was another way I got really close to my students and their families. All their siblings wanted to be what they called "an Oral B. kid." Pretty much all of my kids' younger brothers and sisters asked me, at some point, if they could be part of the foundation. And it always broke my heart to tell them what I knew had to be said, "Unfortunately, it's just this class of kids that gets to be part of the foundation, but I'll tell you what—do your homework, keep your grades up, and do everything you need to do. And when the time comes, if you get ready to go to college and there's no money for you to go, I'll find a way for you to go."

It broke my heart to say that because I knew deep down that without the support network my kids had, most of these other kids wouldn't be able to make it through high school with the grades and the focus they needed to get into college. But it was my hope that maybe if I did a good job with their older brothers and sisters, then they'd be able to serve as role models for the younger generation. And in fact many of those kids who asked me about the program all those years ago have come back and told me about their progress, and asked me for advice about how to continue their education when they get ready. I've told them that my door is always open, and that I haven't forgotten the promise I made to *them*, either.

Unfortunately, I didn't get nearly as much support as I would've liked from my kids' parents. Like I've said, I guess most of them were too harassed by the demands of daily life, like getting something to eat on the table every night, to give their kids the love and support that they needed. Of course, some parents were wonderful, particularly the grandparents. A number of my kids were being raised by their grandmothers, and in general these older women were more settled, established, and informed about what their kids were up against than were the parents. Two grandmothers in particular, Eloise, who was Tracy Easterling's grandmother, and Granny, who was Susan Richards's grandmother, were just ideal. They understood what I was trying to do. They appreciated what I was trying to do. And it showed. They came along on every outing and pitched in however they could—bringing food to our picnics, packing goody bags for the kids on Halloween.

So that's how I started to bond with my kids and get to know about their daily lives. We had lots and lots of fun. For us, fun didn't have to do with material things—it could be as simple as organizing a game of tug-of-war on the playground at recess. Or sometimes, on picnic days, the kids would like to wrestle me if I threatened to keep their food away from them. All of a sudden eight or ten little bodies would jump on me and wrestle me to the ground! It sounds brutal, but when I got up I'd be sputtering with laughter. Then I'd get them their bologna sandwiches and potato chips, and we'd all sit together on the grass like we were eating at a king's table. Then, when Mrs. Waters came out to the playground to get them, they'd all run off, yelling, "We love you, Mrs. Brown!" To this day, one of my favorite meals is just a bologna sandwich and some potato chips.

But the crucial purpose of my presence at Brookfield was to monitor the kids' educational progress in the classroom. I'm very proud to say that none of my kids fell behind during elementary school. They had excellent teachers throughout their elementary school years and I made sure that they had the best Brookfield had to offer in terms of everything else. How did I do that? I hollered and made a fuss when the kids needed textbooks, or art supplies, or maybe just the opportunity to get the school television for an hour so that they could watch a science video.

We didn't necessarily get all of these things—Brookfield was cash-strapped just like every other public school in a low-income neighborhood, and there had to be enough for all the other students, too. But I'll say this: I found the old adage that the squeaky wheel gets the grease to be true throughout my experience with my babies. Since I was down there in Principal Peeks's office telling her what our class needed, she was more likely to remember our needs when it came time to distribute the resources. My kids definitely had things in their classrooms that other kids at Brookfield didn't have.

Some of that came from the fact that they had extraordinary teachers, all dedicated to the point that they would buy lots of things out of their own pockets. But a lot of it is due to the fact that I kept up a running dialogue with the administration. Once again, that's a simple thing that every parent can do for his or her child. Let the principal know that there are shortages in your child's classroom, or that your child needs certain things to learn, and keep making the point. You're likely to see something happen.

I had good working relationships with all of my babies' elementary school teachers. We were lucky enough to keep Mrs. Waters for three years—she had those kids for first, second, and third grade. I would've had Mrs. Waters teaching my kids all the way through high school if she could have. She was just a remarkable teacher, the type of teacher who only comes along once in a kid's lifetime. She had concern for her students that I hadn't seen since I was a kid myself, sitting in Miss Grace's classroom in Mississippi.

Sometimes I would walk into Mrs. Waters's classroom and she'd be in the middle of telling them something like, "My kids are the best students at Brookfield, and you'd better not listen to anyone who says anything else!" She really made it a point of pride to instill confidence in my babies, to make them believe that they really were the best society had to offer. She knew that they would get a lot of negative messages after they left her class, so she tried to fortify them with positive thinking about who they were now and who they could grow up to be. She was just a great, great teacher. We still talk today, and even though she's been retired for years, she remembers the names of all of the babies and asks about each of them.

So you can imagine that I was awfully sad to say good-bye to Mrs. Waters at the end of third grade. Even though I knew Mrs. Peeks had made a special exception to let Mrs. Waters teach my kids for as long as she did, I did try one more time to keep her teaching my kids. "She's got such a bond with those kids," I remember pleading to Mrs. Peeks. "Can't she just keep them for one more year?"

"First of all, Mrs. Waters doesn't teach the fourth grade," Mrs. Peeks said. "Second of all, it's probably bad for the kids not to have the experience of another teacher. How else are we going to get them ready for middle school? Besides, Mrs. Brown, you have to be generous. Give some other kids the opportunity to have Mrs. Waters as a teacher."

Grudgingly, I agreed to let my kids move on. Mrs. Peeks was probably right with all of her reasons—but I wasn't happy about it, and I let Mrs. Peeks know that. "I'm glad that you've enjoyed working with Mrs. Waters," was her reply. "Have you thought a little bit about the fourth-grade teachers we do have?"

Fortunately, I had foreseen this. Right before the third-grade school year was over, I had had a conversation with Mrs. Waters about where my kids should go next. "Come on, Mrs. Waters," I said. "You know these teachers. Who's going to be the best one for my kids?"

I knew that was the right move when she started going over each fourth-grade teacher in detail. They were all *okay*, she said, but some of them were more okay than the others. Her vote was for a teacher named Robert Webb, who was patient and thorough when it came to teaching different subjects and, importantly, knew how to enforce discipline in the classroom. I listened to Mrs. Waters carefully—I respected her opinion more than anyone else's at the school. And I would definitely advise all concerned parents to do what I did. Once again, it's just a simple thing that makes a big difference: check out the reputations of your kid's possible teachers. When you hear that a particular teacher is good, make sure that your kid gets in that classroom. It can mean the difference between your kid learning something that year or falling behind.

"I'd like for my kids to go to Mr. Webb's classroom," I told Mrs. Peeks. "Do you think we can make that happen?"

"I think we can," Mrs. Peeks said.

At the beginning of the school year, I knocked on Mr. Webb's classroom door and proceeded to do what I continued to do with every one of my kids' teachers throughout the program. I introduced myself and asked him if he'd heard about the foundation. He had, so I told him, "I'm not here to interfere with your teaching. I'm here to help."

"Well, you must know that I can use that," he said. "I can use all the help you can give."

"I figured," I said. "I've never met a teacher who couldn't use some help. So we're on the same page. And that's good, because you'll be seeing a lot of me."

I told Mr. Webb that I had general access to the school and would be stepping in once or twice a week, not to spy on him, but to help out and check on my kids. "Mrs. Peeks told you that you'll have twenty-three kids, but just count on having twenty-four," I told him.

He smiled. "I'll keep that in mind." I gave him all of my phone numbers and said that he should feel free to use them in the case of any problems.

But we didn't really have any problems in elementary school. Mr. Webb was, as Mrs. Waters had predicted, a great teacher. So was the fifth-grade teacher that he suggested for the kids to go to next, a woman named Alma Finch. I loved Mrs. Finch in the same way that I had loved Mrs. Waters — once again, she was a woman who had a deep concern for her students. With all of us working together, we got those kids through elementary school with all of them right on track academically. And fortunately, no one had any dire family problems in elementary school. That made things a lot easier.

That's not to say that the seeds of future problems to come weren't already there. If anything about those early years surprised me, it was that my kids were so vulnerable. I truly felt that my kids loved me within about a year of coming to know me. Within a year—and I really didn't do that much. I really didn't. Because, if you take away the financial part of my adoption—if someone had told them I was putting away $10,000 a year for them, they wouldn't have understood what that meant or what kind of sacrifice that took—they just loved me for spending time with them.

When I walked into Mrs. Waters's classroom, I remember twenty-three little faces swiveling toward me, and all of those faces would just spark up like lightbulbs. "Miss Brown!" they'd whisper, even though Mrs. Waters would be thundering above them, "Pay attention, class!" They'd be trying to get my attention while Mrs. Waters was telling them to do the opposite thing. And even though I'd point to the teacher, I'd be laughing inside.

"Miss Brown!" they'd whisper, and I'd see their little hands snaking up beside their desks, trying to wave to me, even though it would get them in trouble. And it was that kind of enthusiasm that let me know I was on the right track and that I had done the right thing to adopt these kids. Because I hadn't had any experience with kids outside of my own family, for a while there I was really questioning myself. But after that first year it became clear, as far as the kids were concerned, that we were all on the right track.

There were always so many things they wanted to share

with me, so many stories to tell, so many games to play. I was amazed at how appreciative they were of their mysterious new friend, and how open they were to sharing everything about their lives with me.

But I knew that I had a hard road ahead of me. For one thing, I started to feel a time crunch as the kids got older. As I learned more about the real estate business, I built up a clientele. More and more people offered me listings and commissions. That's good, because that meant that I was doing a good job with my business, but it was hard at the same time because there was more and more work to do at the school.

As the kids moved on to fourth and fifth grade, their lessons got more complex, their social interactions with other kids got more intense, and it quickly became clear that I was needed more than ever. All I could do was grit my teeth and keep my commitment to spending time at Brookfield once or twice a week. Sometimes it meant losing a business opportunity, but it's never been about money for me. The kids always came first.

The other thing that let me know we were in for a long road ahead were the monthly parent meetings. I held a parent meeting on the second Tuesday night of each month, between 6 and 8 p.m. There was no real agenda for these meetings, just an update from the teacher on each of the students and an opportunity for the parents to ask questions. Occasionally I'd organize a potluck, too, for no particular reason other than that I thought it was a nice idea.

I insisted on the monthly meetings because I wanted to see the parents. I wanted to know what was going on in the home, and I wanted the parents to know what was going on in the school. None of them belonged to the Parent-Teacher Association, so it was maybe the only way for me to see how active they were in their kids' lives. And the answer I got from those meetings was troubling. First of all, not nearly enough of the parents actually showed up to these meetings. I'm not going to name names, but certain people *always* had an excuse. I understand how it is when you're working hard. But you can't *ever* get some time off of work to check in on how your kid is doing in school? That's not a scheduling problem, that's a different kind of problem. And that was the kind of problem that I was going to be faced with throughout my time with these kids.

Through those meetings, I also learned about the kids' different family situations. Most of them lived with only their mothers and didn't have much contact with their fathers. A number of them lived with grandmothers, or grandparents, even if their mother was still around. Sometimes it would be a situation where the kid and his mother were living in the same house with the mother's parents and a number of aunts and uncles. Most of them moved frequently; someone always had a new phone number at every meeting.

So I learned that there wasn't a lot of stability in the kids' familial situations, which usually is a sign that the kids will have a hard time getting their homework done and focusing on their schoolwork in general. That was mildly disturbing, and it was certainly a tremor of things to come, but what troubled me most was how apathetic some of these parents felt about their kids' education. I've mentioned how when I started the program, no one had started saving for college yet. All parents need to start saving that money as soon as their children are born. Okay, so they hadn't done that, but that was about money, and I understood that these parents were struggling. What I didn't understand was why none of these parents seemed to have time for their children. It shocked me that, with a few exceptions, most parents weren't even interested in getting involved with the kids' education at Brookfield!

I'm going to say a few words about this for the parents who are reading this book, because it's a topic that's dear to my heart. *It is not that hard to make a big difference in the quality of education your child receives.* All it takes is the investment of a little bit of time. And it doesn't matter if you're a high school dropout yourself, or if you think you're dumb—everybody can contribute something. If you're old enough to be a parent, you're old enough to have learned something that will be of value to the children in the classroom. Even if it's no more than knowing how to stack the books up at the end of class or putting the chairs up on the desks after school. Get involved. Do something.

And I know it sounds trite, but the technique that Joe Brown used in *Lean on Me* really works—he insisted that his high school students clean up their school. In the case of an elementary school, I'd put it on the parents rather than the students: get out there on weekends and paint over all that graffiti. Plant some bushes and sweep the playground. It makes a big impression on the kids and it builds their self-esteem. No one, no matter how motivated, is going to feel anything but depressed if he or she has to enter a school that's full of trash and covered with nasty graffiti. And it really doesn't take a lot of time or money to beautify a school.

Nor does it take a lot of time to keep your kid learning in

the classroom. The quickest way to do that is to do what I did—spend a couple of hours a week at the school, and let your kid know before you go that you're going to be there. There will be a lot less nonsense from your kid about how the teacher hates him or her, and a lot more interest in being attentive to what the teacher's saying. Or, if you can't spend a couple of hours a week, take a day off of work every once in a while. Spend that day in the classroom. If you hated school yourself, you don't have to help out with the math or the science lessons—all teachers need plenty of help in every way you can imagine. So don't let that be an excuse for not being there to help out.

Ultimately, what it comes down to is this simple fact: my kids got lucky with their teachers at Brookfield Elementary School. They had teachers who cared about them and their progress. But most kids aren't that lucky, and most teachers are too stressed out to show individual concern for any kid. So you can't just drop your kids off at school and hope that they'll learn something. They are still your responsibility, even while you're working miles and miles away. And your responsibility for their education starts as soon as they enter school. Because if they fall behind then, they may never catch up.

5

Overcoming Obstacles

When I started junior high school, I felt like I was walking onto a different planet. To some extent, I was: It was the 1950s and I was adjusting to New York, my first desegregated school, my first urban neighborhood. I was working hard for my sister and her family, helping them raise their children. And I missed my mother.

But when I think about my years in junior high school as compared to those of my babies, I can't even imagine. The year my kids entered junior high school, 1992, was the same year of Oakland's highest murder rate to date. Drugs, especially crack cocaine, had stormed their communities. They didn't experience the pain of segregation, at least officially — whether my kids in Brookfield were getting the same books as the kids in the Oakland hills is another discussion. But the violence they had to experience at school was, if anything, more real: several times during these years I had to drive to Madison Middle School in the middle of the day to pick up my kids, because the school had been shut down. The reason? Someone had found out that a student had brought a knife or a gun to school.

Fortunately, none of my babies ever got hurt. If anything, they were excited to get out of school early. They were just kids, you know, and kids don't really understand just how dangerous weapons are. It's probably true that the kids who brought those weapons to school didn't really understand what it means to stab or shoot someone. But I did, and those episodes illustrated to me the difference between their junior high school years and mine. I might have grown up with segregation, but I also grew up with loving parents and extended families and communities. I'm not sure I'd say the same thing about Oakland in the 1990s. There's a difference between growing up with "Community Watch," like my babies did, and growing up with the next-door neighbor looking out for you, like I did.

I grew up in a time where the praises of discipline were sung from every corner and street and classroom and church bell. I don't know if there was any discipline in the society that my babies grew up in, and I'm even less certain that there's any now. So I was feeling a little lost when my babies entered junior high school. Because this was the way that the world was now, for them, and they were just regular adolescents, going through the same things that every adolescent faces: puberty and awkwardness and feeling a need to fit in.

To the best of my knowledge, I think all of my babies had a good time during these years. The foundation certainly did everything we could to make those years good and memorable, and my memories of those years are filled with images of happy, healthy kids. But adolescence is a difficult time, and

I also know that there were lots of things they didn't tell me, things that kids that age just don't want to talk about with adults.

For example—and no one has ever told me this—I'm sure that some of my babies were approached during these years to get involved with drugs. The boys, in particular, must have been approached about selling. It would have happened starting in junior high school and continuing on, for the ones who still live in Oakland, through the present. In elementary school drugs weren't really on the kids' radar screen. All of them lived close enough to their elementary school that they could walk there with an older brother or sister. If they lived more than a couple of blocks away, their parents took them to school. The influences of evil just weren't at hand the way they are when a kid gets old enough to take the bus to a school across town.

But I knew drugs were going to come up, and I didn't waste any time teaching my babies about how dangerous they are. The way I see it, as soon as a kid is old enough to learn the ABCs, he's old enough to learn about drugs. I started talking about them the second time I met with them in first grade.

"Any of you hear about drugs yet?" I asked them. "No? Good. Then I'm going to tell you all you need to know about them, which is that you need to leave them alone."

They didn't have any idea what I was talking about. They were six years old. But I took a few minutes out of nearly every meeting we had in elementary school to explain what drugs were and what they do to people, so that by the time they got to junior high school they didn't feel a need to experiment. I knew that they would need a lot of information about why they needed to stay away from drugs in junior high school, because peer pressure is so strong during those years.

One thing I didn't tell them about—and I'm not sure to this day whether or not it was the right decision—was a drug situation that was going on right under our noses. I hadn't adopted this class for more than a year when someone hinted to me that there was a situation with the family of Winter, one of my babies, that I needed to check out. After I heard that, I started watching Winter more carefully. She was a sweet kid, very loving, and she was never unkempt, but I noticed that she was often absent from school. No one could explain to me why she was always gone, so I decided to ask her mother myself.

So one day after school I stopped by Winter's house. I knocked on the door and waited a long time. Finally, the door opened, and without even going inside the house—which I never did, because I wasn't invited to do so—I smelled some serious marijuana. I mean, it didn't take but a minute to know what was going on.

I wasn't the only one who was concerned, either. Later that year, someone called Child Protective Services to check on Winter. And the social worker took Winter away the same day she made her first visit to that house. She had interviews with a number of people about Winter, including me. She asked me if I wanted to make any suggestions about a new living situation for the child, but I didn't know anything about Winter's family; I didn't know if she had any relatives who were willing to take her; I didn't even know anything about the process. I had no experience with Child Protective Services, the courts, or anything like that.

"I don't really know what I'm doing when it comes to this

kind of thing," I told her. "I just know that I want the child to be in a safe environment, with someone who's not on drugs."

So they put Winter with the Woods family, who later adopted her. And fortunately, there wasn't any fallout with her mother or anyone else. I've since heard about terrible situations with the birth parents and the foster parents fighting over a child, and situations where parents, who clearly aren't fit to take care of a child, refuse to give him or her up. Luckily we didn't get caught up in any of that, but that was my first lesson in the realities of life for my babies. I didn't want to single Winter out, but I started lecturing them early about all sorts of dangers that were waiting for them. I figured that a little early knowledge couldn't hurt. And that way, if any of the kids were in a predicament, maybe they'd be able to recognize it and let me know.

"I don't care who they are," I told my babies, "don't let anybody give you drugs. Don't take them from a policeman, your mama, your daddy, or one of your little friends. If I lose my mind someday and start offering them to you, you still say no. You got that?"

"Yes, Mrs. Brown," they'd all chant in a singsongy voice. They weren't really listening to me. They were bored. They wanted to go outside and run around.

But I was hoping that the lesson would stick in the back of their brains, because when it was time for junior high Mrs. Brown couldn't be there to give them lessons in the classroom anymore. Not only did the junior high years bring adolescence and all the struggles that come with it, but they brought a new sense of isolation. My babies had been in the same classroom together all through elementary school. Now they were spread out among five different junior high schools in Oakland.

Instead of having one teacher all day, they had five or six teachers. They had to learn new routines and make new friends. For some of them, the whole day would go by and they wouldn't even see any of their former classmates. I had to come up with a plan to keep all of us together and focused, and I had to do it quickly.

As soon as I saw where the kids had landed and what their days were going to be like, I knew that my old strategy of spending time with them in the classroom wasn't going to work. Everyone was in a different classroom at different times of the day, and just the thought of running up and down the halls trying to find my students exhausted even me. So I decided that we would have to meet as a group outside school and that I'd have to set up some kind of program to help the kids out with their schoolwork.

When the kids were in elementary school, we'd meet once a month with their parents in a classroom at Brookfield. If we ever needed space for an event, Mrs. Peeks would make a way. For whatever reason, the principal at Madison couldn't offer us any space for meetings, so I started brainstorming about another space for us to meet.

The solution actually came from one of the parents. Jorge's mother knew a man named Mr. Jackson who was the head of the Brookfield Homeowner's Association. Among its other duties, the Homeowner's Association was responsible for a community center on 98th Avenue.

"Why don't we ask him if we can use the Brookfield Recreation Center?" she said. "It's a public space and we're the public."

Sure enough, Mr. Jackson agreed to let us use the center for our bimonthly meetings. The kids and I usually met around four o'clock in the afternoon and stayed until we had gotten all of our business done—which sometimes meant that we had to stay until eight o'clock at night.

"What do you all have to say?" I would ask them when the meeting started. "Come on, talk to me. I don't get to see you very often anymore and I need to know what's on your mind."

You see, I ran these meetings like a roundtable discussion, so that all the kids would get to have their say. Maybe that's why they sometimes went on until eight o'clock! If we were planning an event, I wanted to hear from everybody about where they wanted to go and what they wanted to do when they got there. We'd pick a place, and then somebody wouldn't like it, and so we'd have to talk about that. Or something would be going on at one of the kids' schools, an argument with a teacher, and I'd take the opportunity to turn the discussion into a lesson about dealing with adults—"You're still a kid," I'd say. "Don't forget who's the adult."

That was my method of reinforcing discipline and helping them stay children a little bit longer. This was the early 1990s in Oakland. The reality of the matter was that my babies were watching their peers get swept up in drugs and gang violence. Now, I'm not one to speculate on somebody else's discipline, but my guess is that the kids who were getting involved in those kinds of things didn't show too much respect for their teachers, or any other adults for that matter. That was part of the problem.

So I talked to my babies about all the bad stuff, particularly gangs. "Don't get caught up in colors," I told them. "I don't want to hear anything about what everyone else is doing in your class. If everyone's wearing red, you wear purple." But then I would turn it right around and add, "And if everyone else is laughing at the teacher, you get your book out and you do what you're supposed to be doing." I figured that if their peers saw they were serious about their work, maybe they'd decide that they were "nerds" and leave them alone.

Of course, this was *my* wish, but no kid wants to be a nerd, especially in junior high school. So I never told them to keep away from their classmates or not to make new friends, but I sure did everything in my power to keep them focused. The first thing I did—and probably the most important thing—was to meet with each principal at the beginning of sixth grade. I never established personal relationships with the kids' middle school principals the way I did with Mrs. Peeks, but I grew to have great respect for what they were doing. They were in charge of overcrowded, underfunded schools. They were responsible for motivating their overworked teachers. They had to deal with chronic shortages of just about everything.

Still, I was determined that they get to know me—and my kids. "I know you're dealing with a lot here," I would tell them. "But I've worked too hard with these kids to see the wheels come off now. So let's talk about what we can do for these kids, starting with putting them in the smallest classes that you've got at this school."

Once again, the squeaky wheel got that grease. None of my kids were ever in classes with more than twenty-seven students. Some classes at Madison had thirty-five or forty students—how in the world can you expect a student to learn anything in a class like that? It's all the teacher can do to keep control over a class that big. And any parent can do what I did, it's just a matter of taking ten minutes at the beginning of the year to let the principal know where you stand.

Then I started the process of getting the teachers to recognize my students. At the beginning of the year, I went to the school's open house and met all my kids' teachers. I didn't tell them about the program—instead I told them that I was a "concerned community member" who was looking out for this particular child. I asked the teachers if they would mind sending me the kids' report cards, and I gave them permission slips from the parents so that the teachers would feel comfortable doing so. In the end, some of them did so and some of them didn't do so, but at least they knew who I was. I always got the report cards anyway, from the parents or the kids themselves.

Because it wasn't possible for me to spend time with the kids in their classrooms anymore, I made a pointed effort to go on home visits throughout the year. These weren't formal meetings or anything like that. I had a list of all my kids, and every week or so I'd go down the list and pick out a kid I hadn't seen in a while, call his or her mother and ask if I could drop by. Generally there was no problem, so I would stop by after the kid was home from school, and we'd just talk for an hour or so. With the kids who were doing very well in school, I asked them what was their motivating force. Sometimes I'd do it in an aggressive way, so they'd try to come up with an answer rather than just shrugging it off.

"Why are you doing so well?" I asked. "You're supposed to be in the ghetto. Nobody's supposed to do well here."

"I don't know, Mrs. Brown," they'd say.

Sometimes that frustrated me, because if they didn't have a reason for doing well, they might be willing to turn their backs on all their hard work when the temptation came to do so. And I knew that the temptation to do so would come—in fact, for many of them, it was already here.

It was never easy for them, being in the program. In elementary school other kids were jealous, but for the most part they just wanted to be in the program themselves. In junior high, kids get a little bit older and a little bit more savvy. They know that the way to hurt someone you're jealous of is to make fun of whatever it is that they've got and you want. So my kids, who had to adjust to being split up for the first time since they met one another, also had to get used to hearing taunts as they walked down the hall.

"You think you're special because you're an Oral B. kid?" they'd yell, so that everybody in the school, and probably everybody in East Oakland, could hear. "Huh? Huh? You think you're special?"

And there was nothing I could do about that, even though it hurt me at least as much—probably more—than it hurt them.

"You don't even need to respond to that," I'd say when they told me what was going on. "You just keep walking. If you say something back, you'll just give that person what they want. Ignore them and soon they'll move on to bullying someone else."

Things like that let me know that I had to do everything I could to help the kids stay on track with their studies, because otherwise there would just be too many distractions competing for their attention. Fortunately, around this time I met Mr. Mitchell.

I met Dennis Mitchell through my good friend Joanne

Baker. Mr. Mitchell is a high school tutor, and just when my kids were getting ready to go into the sixth grade, he volunteered to tutor them after school. He's now on my foundation board, and I have to say he was crucial during this very difficult stage of my kids' lives.

Mr. Mitchell set up an informal tutoring program three times a week at the Brookfield Recreation Center. He was there every Monday, Wednesday, and Thursday, from five until seven o'clock in the evening, helping the kids with their math and science and whatever else they needed help with. He bought supplies for the kids out of his own pocket, and sometimes he bought snacks for everyone to share, too.

And it worked. Even though Mr. Mitchell was not a babysitter, some of the kids asked him if they could come to tutoring, just because they didn't want to go home.

"Of course you can come," he said. "You just make sure that you come prepared to work." And he'd make sure that everyone knew how to do their homework, and got it done, before they went home that night.

I did my part, too. At every one of our meetings, I asked the kids if anyone needed help with their homework, or if there was anything in particular that they were struggling with. In general, the subjects the kids had the hardest time with—all the way through high school—were math and science. I asked Mr. Mitchell to focus on those things specifically, and I got a good look at what the kids were facing because one of my babies, Susan Richards, came to my office nearly every day to do her homework and talk to me.

Susan Richards. Without a doubt, she's the best mother hen I've ever known. By this age, my babies were old enough to use the phone and call me if they ever wanted to talk, and I encouraged them to do so. But I wasn't expecting conversation on the level that I got it from Susan, especially in junior high school. Every evening she would call me and, like she was going through a list, give me a report on each kid. She was in *everybody's* business. I don't know how she got them to give her information on what they were doing; because right away she would tell everything to me.

"Well, Tracy was acting up in class again today," she'd say, about Tracy Easterling. Susan *never* liked Tracy, probably in part because Tracy was so loud and proud and had a habit of getting into mischief. But I spent a lot of time with Tracy during junior high, and I knew that part of the reason why she was always drawing attention to herself was because she didn't get a lot of attention at home. Her grandmother, Eloise, was a strong, formidable woman who loved Tracy to death, but her parents were troubled. I think that really affected Tracy, especially since she had a little sister whom she loved more than life itself. She was more worried about the impact her parents were having on her little sister than she was about herself. So Tracy was actually a sweet girl and, at least to me, she was very shy in some ways.

"Tracy, why do I hear you're acting up in school?" I'd ask, and she'd just give me the sweetest little smile. She knew how to be quiet if she wanted to. She was also quiet when she would call me and ask if I would buy her some food.

"Miss Brown, I'm hungry," she'd say.

"What's wrong, baby?" I asked. "You don't have anything to eat at home?"

Silence on the other side of the phone.

"Tracy, can you take the bus down here?" I asked her, and she'd say that she could—I saw to it that all my babies had bus passes. When she came to the office I took her to the supermarket and bought her food, no questions asked.

But I didn't want to share that with Susan. So I tried to find ways of letting her know that Tracy was special, too, without putting Tracy's business in the street.

"Well, Susan, maybe Tracy's just hoping that someone will notice her," I said.

"But you notice her all the time, Miss Brown," Susan said. "You're always spending time with her."

"That's right, because I love Tracy as much as I love you. I spend plenty of time with you, too," I said.

And I did. If Susan wasn't on the phone with me, she was in my real estate office on East 14th Street. During junior high school, she would call me in the afternoons and ask if she could come by the office. As long as I wasn't headed out with clients, it was fine. We set up a little desk for her near the computer, and she sat at that little desk every afternoon and did her homework. Most of the time I was working hard on something else, but if she was having trouble, I'd stop what I was doing and help her. That didn't happen too often, because Susan was a good student and a very smart kid. But it gave me a good opportunity to see the kind of work that all the kids were doing.

When she was done with her homework, she'd play games on the computer, or sometimes she would file paperwork for me. All the while steadily talking about all the kids and what they were up to. I'd sit at my desk, working hard at all my paperwork, and biting my tongue to keep from giggling. A person is going to tell you news the way that *they* see it, and if Susan didn't like one of the kids she never had anything good to say about them. But I was happy that she wanted to share. I never asked her why she wanted to spend all this time with me, and she never volunteered a reason. It wasn't important. I was glad that she thought enough about me to want to spend her afternoons at my office. And I was happy that I could be there to listen to her.

So I would say that I spent more time with Susan than probably any other kid during these years, although it wasn't because I favored her over any of the other ones. The other kids were busy with other things, and the best way I could monitor their grades was through the tutoring program. I'm very fortunate that Mr. Mitchell showed up when he did, because otherwise there wouldn't have been any way for us to know if someone was falling behind until it was too late. I went to every parent-teacher night and every open house, but other than that the only way for me to learn what was going on in the classroom was by listening to the students—who, let's face it, weren't necessarily going to tell me what was going on—and by looking at their report cards. Sometimes by the time you get the report card, it may already be too late.

So Mr. Mitchell and I developed a strategy to stop any possible problems before they snowballed. The first red flag shot up if we heard a kid complaining about a teacher. If a kid is doing well in a class, he or she loves that teacher. You'll never hear a bad word about a teacher unless something's going wrong. So if I heard that, or if Mr. Mitchell heard that and told me, I'd head right over to the school and have a meeting with the teacher.

"Is there anything I should know about?" I'd ask the teacher. "Any reports, any problems, bad grades? How are *you* doing? Have you ever noticed anyone having trouble understanding the lesson?"

I'm no fool — I know that sometimes my kids were just complaining about a teacher — but I also know that sometimes they had teachers who didn't know how to teach. So if we got a situation like that, that's when Mr. Mitchell and I stepped it up with the tutoring program. I told the kid, in no uncertain terms, to be at the Brookfield Recreation Center every week to get some help.

"I don't want to hear any complaints," I'd say. "Just make sure you're there." I'd also talk to the parents, to let them know what was happening and to try and get their support. Most of them were very supportive of keeping their kids in a tutoring session after school, rather than letting them run around the neighborhood with no supervision.

I think the presence of Mr. Mitchell was also a real bonus because he offered the kids, especially the boys, a male role model. Girls can look up to their teachers if they need to know that it's okay to be smart, and most kids have a mother who tells them they need to do well in school. But it's harder to find men who are pushing that same message, especially as teachers.

Besides, I was starting to realize that I couldn't do it all by myself. The time crunch had started toward the end of the kids' elementary school years, as I got settled into my real estate business and had to cope with increasing demands on all sides. During junior high school, it got even worse. I had new challenges to deal with, both personal and professional.

I launched a new business in 1991. It was two businesses,

actually: I had a full-service restaurant, Cobblers, on East 14th Street near 88th Avenue, and I had a contract with ten California military bases to provide them with frozen peach cobblers. We made the peach cobblers in the restaurant, after business had shut down for the night, and we shipped them to the bases by frozen freight.

Now, the typical reaction people have when I tell them about this five-year period of my life is that they throw up their hands.

"What? Were you out of your mind? With everything else you had going on, you decide to take on a brand-new business?"

And the answer I give them is, yes, I did, and it was a nightmare. A complete nightmare. The restaurant was open six days a week, Tuesday through Sunday, from 6 a.m. to 10 p.m. Seaside Freight came to pick up the cobblers twice a week for delivery to the military bases, so when they came by we had to have five hundred frozen cobblers ready and waiting for them. I didn't have a business partner, and the staff of the restaurant was just two cooks and three waitresses during the day. And then there were five people who came in at night to help me make the cobblers.

So this is what my days started to look like while my babies were in junior high school: I would work at the restaurant from around 5 a.m. to 9 a.m. And when I say work, I mean *work*: yes, I was doing paperwork and managing the staff, but on most mornings I was also doing the cooking for the breakfast shift, because the first cook didn't come in until 9 a.m. Some mornings I was even busing the tables, if one of the waitresses had called in sick.

Around 9 a.m., when the cook came in, I left the restaurant and drove over to my real estate office. I worked at the real estate office from 9 a.m. until around 5:30 p.m., and then I got back to the restaurant around six for dinner. We closed at ten, and then I helped the staff clean up and close the restaurant down before the peach cobbler staff came in around midnight. The peach cobbler shift went from midnight until we got the cobblers done, which sometimes meant we were there until six in the morning.

As to when I slept, the answer is that I didn't. I grabbed an hour here or a couple of hours there, whenever I could find a break. My brother EQ and I had become very close in the late 1980s, and he was of tremendous help to me during the early years of the restaurant. There were many, many occasions when he came to the restaurant around six in the evening and forced me out the door.

"Go home," he'd tell me, and sometimes he'd even be half-dragging me to my car. "Go to bed. I'll take care of this shift and I'll help them close up. Now get out of here." And then he'd stay and take care of the restaurant until they had to close everything up. Some nights I would come back to the restaurant after they'd closed it, to help out with the cobbler shift, and sometimes I didn't. After a couple of years I didn't have to go in for the cobbler shift so often anymore, because I found an excellent manager, an older woman from the South, who understood what I was trying to do and made it her mission to make sure every cobbler that was leaving the building with the Oral Lee Brown trademark was up to my standards.

And what was I trying to do, exactly? Well, to be honest, I wasn't trying to run a restaurant. Cobblers became a neigh-

borhood institution in the five years that it was open. Everyone who was anyone in Oakland, from the mayor to the
Raiders players, ate there at some point. Whenever someone
important was passing through Oakland, somehow they always got the suggestion to eat at Cobblers, and that's how I finally got to meet the man who provided the sound track to my
childhood, B. B. King.

We never did any advertising, either—I don't mean to toot
my own horn, but the food I was serving at Cobblers was quite
simply the best in town. On Sunday afternoons, when we
served turkey and dressing, there was always a line stretching
down the block. We ran out of certain dishes sometimes by
eight o'clock in the evening, and people would whine and cry
and throw fits right in the restaurant! Then they'd swear that
they wouldn't come back, but the next week they'd be in line
again.

So the restaurant was successful, but to tell you the truth I
never wanted to run it in the first place. I only opened the
restaurant because I had a government contract to sell the
cobblers, and I *did* want that contract. If I hadn't had that contract with the government, I would have had to try getting
shelf space at a major supermarket chain like Safeway, and I
had already researched my options there. They wanted
$53,000 to give me shelf space for my cobblers at Safeway, and
that just wasn't an option. The military bases were my best
bet.

My government contract would have allowed me to provide
cobblers to every military base in the northwestern United
States. But at the same time, it stipulated that I couldn't oper-
ate the cobbler business out of my home as I had originally

planned. I had to have a free-standing business. So that's how the restaurant got started, out of my desire to get my peach cobblers on the market.

That desire is what drove me during these years. It sure wasn't money! Business was good with both the cobblers and the restaurant—I sold about a thousand cobblers a week, and on Sundays the restaurant could easily clear $2,000—but when you add it all up, and subtract your bills, it's really not enough money to justify all that hard work. The real reason I started the business was the same reason that I pushed forward with my real estate business, the same reason that I dedicated myself to these twenty-three kids: I knew it needed to be done, and I knew that I could do it.

For all of my life, I'd been going into grocery stores, and I'd never seen anyone's face that looked like mine on a product, other than Aunt Jemima and Uncle Ben. And neither Aunt Jemima or Uncle Ben count, because looking at the faces on those products made me feel worse about myself rather than better. So for all of my life, I'd been thinking about why this was, when the best food I'd ever eaten in all my life always came from a black cook? Why weren't those black cooks getting their products in Safeway, or Albertson's? Why didn't they have restaurants around the world like McDonald's does?

Now, of course I learned the answers when I got older: black cooks, and black communities for that matter, have never had the money, the access, or the business savvy that it takes to really push your product on the mass market. But just because I learned the answers doesn't mean I accepted them. I'd been cooking peach cobblers with my mother's recipe for years. I knew that my cobblers could whup Sara Lee in a taste test any day of the week and twice on Sunday. So from childhood on, I had this dream about getting my cobblers out there, and one day I just decided, today's the day that I need to get working on this if I ever plan to do it.

It just so happened that that day occurred when I had all these other things going on, but I didn't let that stop me. It probably wasn't the *best* time for me to launch another business, but it was the first time in my life that I felt I had enough money and enough knowledge to go after my dream. If I hadn't done it then, who knows if I ever would have? It was very, very difficult, but it would've been even more difficult for me to not do something that I believed in. When I feel strongly about something, there's no limit to what I'll do. Sleep, personal time, material things—all of them can just get pushed aside if I feel that I have to do something on principle.

I didn't achieve my ultimate dream. There was no way that I could have come up with $53,000 to get on the same shelf as Sara Lee. I didn't even have the capital or the manpower to supply cobblers to all the military bases that I could have. I would have needed to employ one hundred people for that, and we would have had to work seven days a week to make enough cobblers for all the military bases in the Northwest. I only did ten bases in Northern California.

But I did achieve my goal. Everybody on the military bases that I did serve knew about Oral Lee's frozen cobblers. They knew about them and they liked them. The orders kept coming in. Those orders told me that I was right, that the cobblers were, in fact, good enough to be on the mass market. If I had had the money and the energy to make the cobbler business my main enterprise, I'm sure that I could have eventually taken them to the mass market. And whupped Sara Lee in that taste test.

In the end, though, it became too much. The restaurant, especially, got to be too much—Cobblers was only in operation for five years, but during that time we had seventeen break-ins. The seventeenth time it happened was in 1996, at the beginning of March. The guys that did it came in around nine o'clock at night, right after I had left the building. My daughter Phyllis came in during the dinner shift to relieve me, saying that she would help out for the rest of the evening if I went home and got some rest. I told her that I would go home and lie down for maybe an hour, and then I'd be back to help them close the restaurant. Phyllis had helped me out before, but she wasn't familiar with everything the way that EQ and I were.

Now, I don't know if these guys were just waiting for me to leave or what, but as soon as I got home I heard the phone ringing. When I picked it up, all I could hear was my daughter on the other line, and she was screaming bloody murder. I couldn't get her to calm down and tell me what had happened, and hearing her scream like that made the hair on the back of my neck stand up. So I hung up the phone and called an old friend of mine who lived about two blocks from the restaurant.

I called him because if my baby was hurt, I needed someone to get there quick. Now in ordinary places the first place you should call is the police station, but I knew the police in Oakland. In those days, if you called the police in Oakland and told them that someone had been shot, it took them thirty minutes to show up. So I called the person who I knew would get there in a timely fashion.

"Something's happened," I said when he picked up. "Something bad. I don't know what's going on down there, but you have to go right now and find out. And as soon as you find out, you call me."

"I'm rolling, right now," said my friend, and he hung up the phone.

I paced around my house for about ten minutes. I was too scared to go down to the restaurant myself, but after about ten minutes passed and I didn't get another phone call, I became too scared to stay in the house either. So I grabbed my purse and drove over there, and as I drove by all I saw were sirens flashing and ambulances and police cars . . . traffic was backed up for blocks.

I parked my car about three blocks away and walked toward the restaurant very, very slowly. I couldn't make out what was going on with the ambulances or the police cars, so I walked inside the restaurant . . . disaster. Glass everywhere, smashed all over the ground in ugly twisted pieces. The whole place was a mess. One of the waitresses was on the ground, screaming, with medical personnel all around her. I nearly fell down myself, but that mother's instinct saved me again.

"Phyllis!" I shouted. "Phyllis!"

And Phyllis was there. She was sitting on the ground with some policemen and medical folks around her.

"I'm here, Ma!" she shouted. "We're all right. Everybody's all right. It's okay."

Thank God, because it very easily could not have been

okay. Shortly after I left, the robbers came in with a shot-gun. Just as plain as day, they walked in, pulled out a shot-gun on one of the waitresses, and demanded to have "the money."

That was my waitress Jamillah, who had to be taken to Highland Hospital that night because she was hysterical. She started screaming as soon as she saw the gun, screaming about how she didn't have the money, that it was at the cash register, and they ran right over to Phyllis, who happened to be stand-ing behind it.

"Give us the money," they said, shoving the gun in her face.

"And Ma," said Phyllis, "I wasn't even scared for myself. All I could think about was, Who's going to take care of my daughter? What's going to happen to her?"

As soon as I heard her say that, I knew it was over. There are some things that are even more important to me than prin-ciple, and in this case, it was my daughter.

Fortunately, Phyllis got the cash register open and gave them the money. At least the fool holding the gun wasn't jumpy, and so, thank God, nobody got shot. They ran away, and one of the waitresses who hadn't already lost it called the police. But everyone else in the restaurant was yelling and screaming . . . even Phyllis took about ten minutes to calm down. She had called me when she was still screaming.

I took a look at my daughter, and then I took a look at poor Jamillah, who was being escorted out to one of the ambu-lances. I looked at the restaurant. Phyllis stood up and I put my arms around her.

"Come on, baby," I told her. "Let's deal with this and get out of here."

And that was exactly what we did. That was early March, and by March 31 we had shut the restaurant down for good. It just wasn't worth it anymore.

There were a lot of reasons why I decided to close Cobblers for good. EQ had died the year before. He had a sudden heart attack and died. He was just worn out. I guess somewhere in the back of my mind I realized that he was getting older and that he wouldn't be with me forever, but I had always pushed those thoughts away. After all, I had only gotten to know him when we had gotten older, and then he was so delightful that I couldn't dream of being without him. Not only did he help me out at the restaurant, coming in for the dinner shift, but he was my friend, my confidant, and my advisor. When he died, it broke my heart.

EQ had been there for me in 1995, too, when my marriage to Joe ended. I don't even know what to say about my breakup with Joe Brown, the nicest man I've ever met. A lot of people ask me if I sacrificed my marriage for the Oral Lee Brown Foundation. The answer is yes. I can understand why they'd ask that question, because I made my promise right after my own children left the house. That's exactly the time when many couples are winding down their outside commitments, and finally taking the chance to get to know each other again. Still, I wouldn't say that Joe and I broke up because I was spending so much time looking after my babies. We had our own problems, and we would have had those problems regardless of how much time I was spending with the kids. But it was still hard being without him, and I realized that again as I walked into my ruined restaurant.

EQ was gone. Joe was gone. And now I had almost lost

Phyllis, too, and over some fool who was trying to rob us for a couple of hundred dollars? No, no, and no. I said enough is enough, and I closed Cobblers down.

It was sad. It was sad for me to have to shut down my dream, but it was even sadder for the city of Oakland. Every single one of those break-ins was done by an African-American, or a group of African-Americans. Most likely all of them were locals who didn't live but a few miles away. They'd probably gone to Brookfield and Madison and Castlemont, just like my daughters had, just like my babies were doing at that exact time. And what they didn't know was that every single time they broke into Cobblers to steal a couple of dollars or some food from me, they were stealing from themselves. I started that restaurant so that they would have a decent place to eat in their own neighborhood. I started the cobbler business so that one day they could go into a supermarket and see someone that looked like them on a product. And they were just destroying their own opportunities.

But that's what happens when poor people don't get a proper education and some self-respect. So while I was sad and hurt that I had to close up my restaurant and my cobbler business, the experience just made me focus even more on what I was trying to do with my babies. Those men who felt that they were grown enough to hold a shotgun up to somebody's face weren't much older than they were. And I knew that those men had struggled with the same tough neighborhoods and the same hard choices that my babies were struggling through right now.

I didn't tell my babies about the robbery. I didn't want to scare them. But as they finished junior high and got ready to start high school, I looked at them with more concern than ever. For all I knew, those robbers could have been in the same position my babies were: smart young kids who got caught up in the need to hustle themselves a living. Who was to say that I had what it took to stop it from happening again?

6

Staying Motivated:
How the Kids Got Into College

During the fall of 1996, I wrote the following letter to several colleges around the state and the country: "To whom it may concern, Please send me your latest undergraduate application. I would also appreciate it if you sent me your school's eligibility requirements." Within a few weeks the information booklets were pouring in.

While my babies were starting the ninth grade at Castlemont and Skyline high schools, two of the roughest schools in Oakland, I was paging through college applications and eligibility requirements. I looked through the information carefully, taking notes, and when I had finished with all of the applications I studied those notes to see what those colleges required—in other words, what my job was going to be for the next four years. I was in for a big surprise.

"Extracurricular activities?" I said, scratching my head.

"Community service? SAT scores? *List the financial assets of your parents?*"

I may as well have been reading a foreign language.

I had recently gone to college myself, but I had applied through a special continuing-education program. Besides, that was in the early 1980s, and things had changed in the world of higher education since then. My application hadn't demanded that I turn over my SAT scores and a statement about my achievements in the community. This was obviously going to be harder than just making sure that the kids got good grades.

The colleges were asking their applicants for not only grades and test scores, but lots of other things, too: extracurricular activities, leadership, letters of recommendation, and, of course, money. I expected the money requirement, at least. I knew we would have to hustle up as many grants and scholarships as we could, in addition to using the money that I had been faithfully depositing in the Home Savings Bank.

But the other requirements were unfamiliar, and they made me snap right to attention. We were going to have to get on the ball if we wanted to tackle this in time for the kids to make their applications senior year.

To keep calm, I concentrated first on the requirements that would be easy for my babies to meet: the academic requirements. The first thing I learned was that the requirements for high school graduation and the eligibility requirements for college are *not* necessarily the same thing. For example, a high school may only require students to take three years of math in order to graduate. Nearly every four-year college requires applicants to take four years.

Fair enough. At our first meeting in September, I told the

kids, "I don't care what they tell you at your school about what you need to do to graduate. You have to do more if you want to get into college, and that's what we're going to do here. Now, I'm going to pass out a list of the classes you need to take to graduate with the Oral Lee Brown Foundation, and every semester we're going to check in and see how you're doing."

When the kids started grumbling, I said, "Don't even start," and I passed out the list: four years of math, science, English, and history; at least two years of a foreign language; one semester of civics . . . and we checked in every semester to make sure the kids were taking all the classes they needed.

"You got your civics requirement?" I asked them, or "How come I don't see math on your schedule here? You just didn't get a chance to add it yet, right?"

I never even checked to see what the high schools' requirements for graduation were. As far as I was concerned, the requirements for college eligibility were the requirements for my babies to graduate from high school.

And after a few moments of panic, I got the kids in line with the other requirements, too. Since community service kept popping up on the college applications as either an eligibility requirement or a very favorable activity, I gathered that my babies needed to be doing community service. So I announced it as a requirement at that very same meeting in September.

"And here's where you have an advantage over those kids in the Oakland hills, who are all out there trying to do the same thing," I told them, to shut down any protests. "Because they're all rich up there. Their community programs don't need any help. But you and I both know it won't be hard to find people who need help in East Oakland."

It sure wasn't, and we didn't even know a thing about how to set up ways for the kids to get involved with community service. I started out by sending them to my church, First Love Missionary Baptist on 98th Avenue. If they happened to attend a different church, I told them to go there and ask about different things they could get involved in. All of the churches were thrilled that the kids wanted to get involved. They had lots of suggestions.

Their first suggestion was that the kids could come volunteer with the church programs. I thought that was a great opportunity, because almost every church has a whole program of events to help poor people. In addition to helping the needy, the kids would really get a chance to learn how to plan events and organize people, which are great leadership skills.

Some of the kids chose not to volunteer with a church, and that was fine too. First Love Missionary Baptist pointed them to other community programs, like local food banks and the YMCA. Later on, many of them told me that they really enjoyed themselves when they were volunteering. I've also said that there's nothing like helping someone with less than you to get your head straight about how blessed you really are.

We also stepped up the tutoring program. Mr. Mitchell was still doing his three days a week, but a few of my board members offered to help out on the days that he couldn't make it. I talked to the people in charge of the Brookfield Recreation Center, and soon we were running five days a week and half a day on Saturday. When the recreation center wasn't available, we held our sessions at the public library.

We got a huge boost for the tutoring program when the kids

were in tenth grade. One day, I picked up a telephone call and heard an unfamiliar voice on the other end.

"Is this Mrs. Brown?" a bright, happy voice said.

"Yes, who's this?" I said.

"My name's Janessa. I'm a student at Wellesley College in Massachusetts, but I'm thinking about taking a year off to do some community work. I was wondering, if I did that, could I work with the kids in your foundation?"

"Well, what would you want to do?" I asked.

"I don't know, maybe I could tutor them or something?"

"Could you," I said. "How soon can you get over here?"

That was Janessa Joffey. She never told me how she found out about the foundation, and I never asked. I've learned that sometimes it's better not to ask too many questions when blessings fall into your lap. And that's just what she was, a blessing.

Janessa Joffey is originally from Piedmont, a community right here in the Bay Area. Her family is well off, and they were able to support her for the full year that she was on sabbatical from college. That freed her up to do lots of work with my babies. She worked mostly with Mr. Mitchell and the tutoring program, but she didn't just do tutoring.

The first thing she noticed was that my babies, like most people, had a tough time with math and science. Advanced math and science can be difficult and abstract, and it was tough for the kids to relate to those classes sometimes. "What am I going to use this for?" they'd say, or, "I don't see why I need to know this. How many equations do *you* come across in the first place, and then how many of *those* are full of letters?"

So Janessa thought the kids might understand more if they

saw how advanced math and science are applicable in real life. She invited students from the University of California at Berkeley to the tutoring sessions—engineering students, computer science students, students who were studying to be rocket scientists, all sorts of students. The Berkeley students gave fun presentations. There was an engineering student who talked to the kids about building bridges using props. There was a computer science student who taught the kids to use numbers in basic computer code. The kids loved that exercise—they got to see how the numbers they punched in made computer programs behave in different ways.

Afterward, the Berkeley students would pitch in to help the kids with their homework assignments. Some of them would keep showing up at the tutoring sessions every once in a while, which came in really handy when the kids were learning geometry and chemistry and all those things.

It was great for the kids to have tutors who were closer to their age, too. They could talk to Janessa and the Berkeley students about college football or dorm life when they got tired of working on their homework. As long as they could figure out their homework assignments, I didn't mind if they took some time out to talk with the college students about other things. It was good that they had mentors, and I was more than happy that the kids were safely inside the recreation center, chatting away, rather than wandering the streets of Oakland.

The board members of my foundation got more involved with the kids during high school, too. By this time the board had grown to eleven people, mostly through word of mouth. Board members would tell their friends that they were having a good time organizing the banquet, or that they liked what we were doing with the kids, and the next thing I knew I'd get a phone call from someone asking if they could join my board.

"Well, I suppose you can send in your references and a statement about why you want to join," I'd tell them, always surprised at the ways that these folks showed up at the door.

Two of my board members, Mr. Mitchell and Jill Nesbit, were involved in the tutoring program. I asked the others if they'd be willing to take on some mentoring responsibilities.

"We've got to get these kids ready for college," I said. "There are twenty-three of them. And I've had a look at those college applications. So I think I'm going to need some of you to pitch in."

Everyone agreed, and I assigned a couple of kids to each board member. In theory, the board members were supposed to be the first line of defense for any problem that the kids might have. I told the kids to give their report cards to their mentors and alert them if they were having trouble with any subject. I told the board members to tell me if the kids told them about any problems they were having, so we could set up special tutoring sessions or schedule a meeting with the teacher.

The board members took up their responsibilities eagerly, and they did an excellent job. They reminded the kids about required classes and community service. They called the kids to find out how they were doing in different classes. Some of them made a real effort to get to know the kids personally, too. One of my board members, Julie Toliver, still treats her kids, and the kids' parents, to breakfast at least twice a year.

In theory, that's how the mentoring program was supposed to work. Now, of course, in practice, the kids were used to coming to me first with everything. That was even truer in high school, because most of the kids were going to Castlemont High School, which is just down the street from my real estate office. Many of the kids walked past my office on their way home from school—what better opportunity to drop in and tell me about what was going on?

So in practice, the kids gave their mentors their report cards—and they made another copy for me, too. The mentors called them to see what was going on, and the kids would call me as soon as they got off the phone. At first I was a little frustrated, because one of the reasons for the mentoring program was to take some of the stress off of me—but then I figured, "You know what, Oral Brown? Your board didn't adopt these kids, you did. And the buck stops with you."

Besides, it made me feel good that the kids trusted me so much that they would still come to me first with everything that was going on in their lives. Most kids in high school don't want anything to do with adults, so to see their affection and appreciation was very touching. They always came to me first, unless, of course, there was a huge crisis.

We had a huge crisis, too. Well, it *could* have been a huge crisis. Fortunately or unfortunately, I didn't know what was going on soon enough to panic. I just remember that it happened in 1997, when the kids were close to finishing their sophomore year in high school.

It started when I got a call from Susan Richards, the "mother hen" of all my babies.

"So what's going on, Susan?" I asked. "How are all my babies? What's everybody doing? You know if you don't tell me, I won't know, so tell me the story."

She seemed subdued. "Oh, you know," she said. "Everybody's getting by."

"Well, I surely know that," I said. "But you didn't call to tell me what I already know."

"I don't know what you know and what you don't know," she said.

I'm not sure where I was—I must have been at one of my jobs, working on something—but I stopped whatever I was doing when I heard that. Susan had *never* been concerned with keeping somebody's business hidden from me. Right then, she was obviously trying to tell me something, but it sounded like she was worried about getting someone in trouble. If something was so serious Susan would try to keep it from me, I knew it had to be a problem.

"Susan," I said quietly, "don't play with me. What are you talking about? What is going on?"

"Robin had the baby," she said.

"*What* are you talking about?" I said.

"Robin had the baby," she repeated.

"I heard you the first time, and I understand the words," I said. "What I don't understand is what you're talking about. What baby?"

"You didn't know?" Susan said.

No, I didn't. I hadn't seen much of Robin over the last four or five months, which should have been a wake-up call. She hadn't been to tutoring in months, and she had missed the last few group meetings we'd had. But now the times that I had seen her came flashing back to me: Robin wearing a big coat, Robin surrounded by three or four of her girlfriends, Robin insisting on staying seated behind a table when I saw her at her house.

"Wow," I said to Susan. "I really didn't know. How long have you known?"

Susan told me that she hadn't known for a long time either. Robin had tried to keep it a secret from everyone until she started showing, and even then she swaddled herself in clothes and tried to avoid conversations. Eventually, of course, it leaked out from a few of her friends and maybe even from Robin herself. But she had wanted to keep this a secret for a long time. Why?

"Have you talked to her?" I asked. "Has she been to school? What is she doing? What is she planning to do?"

"I don't know, Mrs. Brown."

"Well, you know where she is, don't you? I'll go find out what her plans are from her."

And that's exactly what I did. Robin wasn't but a few days out of the hospital when I marched over to her house and rang the doorbell.

"Well, hi, Mrs. Brown," said Robin when I walked in. She looked embarrassed and maybe a little scared.

"Well, hi, Robin," I said. "How are you feeling?"

"I'm okay," she said. "Tired, that's all."

"Well, you'll get used to that," I said. "Where's the baby?"

"She's over there in the bassinet. She's asleep, though."

I walked over and peered into the bassinet. The baby was curled up in a precious brown bundle under a heap of blankets. Robin had tied a little hat on her head, and between the hat and her skin—nothing but dimples—the baby looked like a little old woman. I smiled.

I love kids. Always have. And I wasn't angry with Robin for having the baby, although I was a little angry with her for keeping it a secret from me for all this time. The baby was just a fact, she had a life of her own, and with luck we'd get her thinking about college in a few years, too. As for her mother, we would find a way to get through this, too—*if* she was willing to work through it.

"I won't pick her up, since she's asleep," I said, even though that's exactly what I wanted to do. "I'm sure you're happy to be getting some rest."

"I sure am," she said. Then she ducked her head and added, sheepishly, "I thought you were going to yell at me."

I sighed. "Well, I'm not. I'm not even going to ask you the questions that I'm sure most people want to know, because as far as I'm concerned, it's a little bit late for all that. This was your decision and your choice. Are you happy with the choice you made?"

"I guess so," she said.

"You guess so?"

"Yeah, I am."

"Then I'll support you," I said, and I decided to let that line of questioning drop. From the time they entered junior high school, I had lectured every single one of these kids about sex and birth control as a matter of course. They knew about birth control pills, condoms, AIDS, and sexually transmitted diseases from an early age.

I even brought in teachers for question and answer sessions, so that the kids could learn about these things from someone who knew more than I did. And I distinctly remember what I said to them after one of those question and answer sessions,

"Now you know about ways to protect yourself from pregnancy. So if any of you come up to me one day and say that you're going to have a baby—and yes, I'm talking to the boys, too, because it takes two to make one—it's evidently because you want one."

As these thoughts were going through my head, Robin still looked scared. "What's wrong, Robin?" I asked.

"Mrs. Brown," she said, "can I still be in the program?"

"Are you going to stay in school?"

"Yes, I am," she said.

"Are you going to graduate from high school? Go on to college?"

"Yes."

"Then of course you can stay in the program," I said. "Having a child doesn't mean that you have to drop out of everything. I think your life's going to be a little bit harder, now, though."

"You sure you're not mad at me, Mrs. Brown?"

"Robin," I said, giving a deep sigh, "you had a baby. You had a baby! Why would I be mad at you for that? Am I disappointed, yes. I'm disappointed. It would not have been my choice for you to have a baby at this age. But now that you've made the decision to have one, my feelings about *you* have not changed. Before you had this baby I was willing to do whatever I could to help you move your life forward, and I'm still willing to do that now. So let's sit down and figure out what we can do to keep you on the path to graduation."

That's what we did. I told Robin that my one condition for her remaining in the program was that I was not going to take on the role of a grandmother. I loved the baby as soon as I saw her, of course, but I made it clear that she was Robin's responsibility. I couldn't take on baby-sitting on top of everything else. Besides, the way I saw it, in the long run the best way I could support the baby was to support her mother.

I did step up to help Robin by shutting down some of the negativity that was headed her way. All of my students heard about the baby eventually, of course, and every single one of them had an opinion. They talked about it at group meetings, so I heard them. Some of them approved of her decision, and some of them didn't. When I heard someone grumbling about how she was stupid, that's when I stood up in front of all of them to address it. Fortunately, Robin wasn't present to hear them call her stupid, so I decided to nip it in the bud before she got back.

"Listen up, all of you," I said. "This is the only time we're going to sit here together and talk about Robin. All your gossip needs to end right now. She made a decision to have a baby, and however you may feel about that, it wasn't your decision to make. So if you can't say something good, don't say anything at all."

"We can't even ask her questions about it?" someone asked.

"If you're asking how she's doing, then that's fine," I said. "But if you've got something negative to say, remember that you don't have to take care of Robin's baby. So the way I see it, there are twelve months in a year and that means that you've got six months to mind your business and six months to leave someone else alone. So you just keep any negativity to yourself."

And that was that. I think the other students really sup-

ported Robin as soon as they saw that she wasn't going anywhere. She didn't use her baby as an excuse to drop out of
school. Instead, she got back to school and worked just as
hard at her schoolwork as any of them.

I was so proud of her, and in fact I point to her as an example whenever I hear someone talk about how poor kids don't
have any interest in going to college.

"Look at my baby Robin," I say. "She had a baby at sixteen.
She's as poor as anyone in East Oakland. She could have
started collecting her welfare check and sat down. But she
didn't give up." She graduated from high school just one semester later than her brothers and sisters in the program, and
now she's at American River College.

So if Robin never wanted to give up on our dream of getting to college, none of them wanted to give up. Deep down in
their souls, they always wanted to finish high school and go on
to college. There were some days in high school when I didn't
know if they would make it, though.

On those days I got phone calls, either from one of my babies or their parents. Tears and shouting and anger and
slammed doors on the other side of the phone—"What is going on over there?" I'd ask.

"I don't even know, Mrs. Brown, but you better get over
here," would be the answer.

And I'd sigh. This happened on a fairly regular basis while
the kids were in high school. Some of it, I think, is just what
every high school kid goes through. High school kids are adolescents, their hormones and their emotions are running high,
and their parents never "understand" them. So the kids make
threats about how they're going to run away, or drop out of

school and get a job, or join the circus, or whatever they're going to do.

The difference is, that unlike the kids in the Oakland hills who make threats about dropping out or running away, those options looked a lot more realistic to my babies. That's what all their peers were doing. The situations of poverty and deprivation that were a fact of life in East Oakland forced a lot of Castlemont High School students to look on school as a long, tedious, and uncertain route to a paycheck.

I knew that before the kids started school there, so I always paid close attention to their frustrations. I tried to hear what was really bothering them. If they were on the verge of doing something drastic, I wanted to know it as soon as possible.

I'll give you an example—let's say it's 1996, the year my babies were in the ninth grade. I got a phone call from one of my babies, let's call her Jody. I was sitting in my real estate office around ten o'clock in the morning. The phone rang, and I picked it up.

"Hello?"

"Mrs. Brown, you need to get over here and get Jody," said Jody's mother.

"What's going on?" I said. "Where's Jody? Why isn't she in class?"

"Can't you hear her yelling at me?" said Jody's mother. In fact, I could hear someone hollering in the background. I could hear a number of other things, too, things that sounded like they were hitting the floor and the wall.

"Oh, Lord," I said. "Are you guys fighting? What happened?"

"I don't want to talk about it right now," said Jody's mother. "Because I'll tell you what I think, and that might make her madder, and you know this could go on and on. I think it's best if she just gets out of my house for a little while."

"I'm on my way," I said, and I hung up the phone and got moving. By the time I got to Jody's house, Jody was already outside on the stoop with her lip stuck out. I parked my car and walked over to her.

"Your mama kick you out?" I asked.

"She can't kick me out," Jody said. "I'm *leaving*. And I'm not coming back, either. I'm getting a job and I'm going to take care of myself."

Now here's where I started to roll my eyes—and pay attention at the same time. I knew Jody didn't want to leave her mother. I knew Jody was too young to get any kind of real job, *and* I knew that, deep down, Jody really wanted to graduate from school and go on to college. If she didn't, she wouldn't hold her head up high when she walked by those boys who taunted her for "thinking she's smart," and she wouldn't be at the tutoring program every week trying to figure out her algebra homework.

But I also knew that 102 people were killed in Oakland in 1996. And I knew that even though crack didn't have the hold on the community that it did even a couple of years before, there was no shortage of "jobs" that Jody could have gotten if she couldn't find work at the local gas station.

So I loaded Jody in my car and we drove over to McDonald's. I bought her some hotcakes, and while she ate she told me all about it.

"She's always telling me what I need to be doing, and what

do I see her doing?" she said. She was still sniffling, so every once in a while I passed her a napkin to blow her nose. "Get off the phone, she says, and every time I turn around she's on it. Clean up this house, and she's home all day messing it up. Can't go out with my friends, can't do this, can't do that—"

"Are you done, Jody?" I asked.

"Oh, now you're going to start in on me, too."

"No, I'm not," I said.

"Yes, you are."

"Listen, Jody, I'm not going to fight with you. What I will do, if you don't want to go home right now, is take you with me to my office. We can talk more there."

So we went to the office, and Jody spent the day with me. She stopped crying pretty quickly, and just mumbled about her mother under her breath. While I worked, she did her homework and helped me with some of my paperwork. When the workday was over, I bought her a hamburger and we sat down for another talk.

"How are you feeling now?" I asked.

"She *still* shouldn't be telling me what I need to do if she can't do it herself," she said sullenly. But I knew I had won. She wasn't talking about leaving home anymore. Now I felt comfortable offering my opinion on the situation.

"She's your mother," I said. "And you know what, sometimes she probably is wrong. I don't know whether or not this is one of those situations because I wasn't there to hear the fight. But you know what? She's your mother, it's her house, and you just have to do what she says. Even when you disagree."

"But that's not fair, Mrs. Brown."

"Life's not fair," I said. "It's not fair that I have to work as hard as I do. It's not fair that you're poor. I could go on and on about what's not fair, but the fact is that we've got to find a way to live with all of it. Now, you want me to call your mother?"

"What are you going to say?"

"I'm going to talk to her about getting you home," I said. "And see what we need to do to make that happen."

So I called Jody's mother, who was more than ready to have Jody back home. It was just a matter of getting the two of them on the phone and listening to them say a couple of gruff, loving things to each other — neither of them wanted to apologize in front of me. Then I drove Jody back home in time for her to get a good night's sleep. But I didn't let her out of my car before I got a promise from her to call me the next time she thought about skipping school.

"I will, Mrs. Brown," Jody said. "This morning was just, you know, it was just a rough time."

"That happens, Jody," I said. "But all the same, you call me next time. You can't skip school."

"I know, Mrs. Brown," she said. "I'll be in school tomorrow. And hey, I got my homework done, didn't I?"

They always did get their work done, all of my babies, even if they were being passed back and forth between relatives like Joseph or scrambling for a place to sleep like Jeffery. They amazed me sometimes. I knew that the boys, especially, were constantly hearing about situations in which their peers were involved with weapons and violence, and even though they didn't say much to me, sometimes I could see that weighing heavily on them.

"Nothing's wrong, Mrs. Brown," they'd say at our bi-monthly meetings. "Just working hard, keeping it together."

❦

It was an interesting time to be keeping things together in East Oakland. The entire Bay Area economy exploded during the late 1990s, thanks to innovations in the technology industry. Money was coming in from all over the place, and most people outside of East Oakland thought the Bay Area was having another gold rush.

It may have been a gold rush for some, but certainly not for us. I personally saw some benefits from the technology boom, because the value of real estate all over the Bay Area soared. Even in the flatlands, home prices went up overnight. And there were so many new people coming into the Bay Area that my days got busier than ever before.

As a real estate agent, I had a great time during those years. But the good times didn't roll for everybody. High property values don't mean anything to people who can't afford to buy houses, like my babies and their families. For them, high property values and a tight housing market just meant increases in rent bills. The cost of living went up to the point where a lot of poor people got squeezed out of the Bay Area altogether. For those who were left, the technology industry didn't bring any jobs for them. If anything, the "new economy" made their lives a lot tougher. Crime was down, but that didn't mean I was less worried that my students would be tempted by the streets—if only to help their families make ends meet.

Sometime in 1996, I started thinking about how I could help my babies see just how close they were to getting a future that *would* allow them to participate in the kind of economic boom they were watching happen all around them. After talking to lots of people, including my board members and Janessa, I decided that a college tour would be a good way to keep them focused. Out of sight, out of mind—college wouldn't be real to them until they actually saw some college campuses, preferably full of people who looked like them.

I bought a book called *College Tours*. And I felt like I'd sent away for those college applications all over again. Planning a college tour can be very complicated, and a lot of the information about procedures and visiting times was overwhelming. Just like there's a whole industry dedicated to getting wealthier kids into college, there's a whole industry dedicated to showing them around on college tours. But since I didn't have access to that, I had to learn the rules myself.

Fortunately, I knew exactly where I wanted us to go. I've always been a big fan of southern colleges, especially the historically black colleges and universities like Spelman, Tuskegee, Xavier, and Florida A&M. I've noticed that graduates from the southern schools have learned a lot more than academics. They've learned pride and confidence, too, and most of them carry themselves with great dignity. It's like they're saying, "I *know* I have a place at this country's table!"

I wanted my babies to see that. Ideally, I wanted at least *some* of my babies to go to these colleges, too. So I zeroed in on a list of historically black colleges in the Deep South, and then I got down to the hard part: organizing the trip, and, of course, paying for it.

It took us a year to raise the money for our trip. We got a few private donations, but most of the money came from fund-raisers we held—lots of bake sales and car washes. We hadn't done those things for years, ever since I came to the abrupt conclusion in 1988 that we would never make enough money for the foundation that way. This time it was easier, both because the economy was better and there was less money to raise. The kids were excited, too, about the idea of flying across the country. Most of them had never been on an airplane.

So we held our bake sales and our car washes, and we actually had fun doing it. I also lucked out with our plane tickets. A childhood friend of mine worked for United Airlines, and she arranged for me to have a meeting with some of the decision-makers over there. I asked them for free tickets, but they couldn't quite do that—nineteen of the kids were going, plus me and five of my board members. Even United Airlines couldn't give away twenty-five tickets. What they could do was offer us discounts, which we took. I think we wound up paying $200 per ticket, which was reasonable.

The airline could only offer us discounts on off-peak tickets, so we had to plan our schedule around those times. I researched hotels for every stop we were going to make, begged them for the cheapest rates, and then made sure that they were willing to let us cram four or five kids and a mentor into each room. And then not all of the colleges were open to visitors when we could go, which was during the spring of the kids' junior year . . . so there were lots of logistical headaches.

Every single hassle was worth it, though, if only to experience the moment we boarded that plane. Like I said, many of the kids had never been on a plane before, so they were practically jumping up and down with excitement. They cheered when the plane took off and spent the flight taking pictures out of the tiny airplane windows. They were so happy, and so proud, that I just had to laugh at all the work it had taken to bring them this far. We were in the home stretch now, and who was going to stop us?

The kids loved visiting the colleges. All of them were really entranced by Spelman and Morehouse, the nationally renowned single-sex colleges in Atlanta. Lots of the boys liked Southern University in New Orleans—I think they liked the city of New Orleans, too.

I wish I'd had the opportunity to take them to some of the colleges in my home state of Mississippi, which may sound strange, considering how much I hated living in Mississippi. The fact is that I don't know if enough has changed for Mississippi to be the type of state in which I would choose to live—I don't know if it's possible for enough *to* change there. I *do* believe, and have always believed, that there are some fine colleges in Mississippi. LaTosha Hunter, one of our class's stars, agreed with me. She decided to go to Alcorn State a couple of years later.

When we got back from the college tour, I was satisfied to see that it really had made a difference in the way the kids saw their futures. They were more focused at the monthly meetings and just all-around happier in general. There seemed to be a consensus to work hard and chug on through to graduation. We had already worked so hard to get to this point, and now that it was within reach, no one wanted to mess up.

And no one did. People like to ask me what the secret was. I tell the truth: there was no secret, just a lot of hard work. Sometimes it was just shaking them up a little bit. During high school, I had to sit nearly every one of those kids down for a reminder about what our goal was, because most everyone went through a time when things were looking rough.

"Listen," I'd say, "I know it's hard now. Your family doesn't have any money; you don't know how you're going to eat; you don't have any new shoes. I'll buy you some food. I'll get you some new shoes. They won't be Nikes, because I can't even afford Nikes for myself. But you'll eat, you'll get your shoes, and you'll keep your behind in school. Don't even think about anything else. Now, is that clear?"

And it was clear, even though I had to help some of them all the way through high school. Some of them were more comfortable about it than others. Jeffery, for instance, was a tough one. He never told me what was going on.

I made sure all the kids' college applications were paid for, too. It costs a lot of money to even *apply* to college, much less attend. First, you have to pay to take the SAT test. Nearly every college requires SAT scores from all applicants. Some of them say that the SAT is one of the most important factors they use in judging applications, second only to the grades. They change the test every year, but you can buy all kinds of books to study the sorts of questions that they ask.

In fact, I'd highly recommend doing just that, because those questions are tricky. I asked Janessa to set up a couple of SAT workshops for the kids soon after we got back from the college tour. She did a great job leading them through the questions about vocabulary and geometry and everything else. The kids spent a whole bunch of Saturdays with some of her old SAT books and the donations she got from the library. If you don't have a lot of money, most libraries have SAT books, or they know where you can find them.

All the kids took the SAT, and I encouraged all of them to take it again if they were willing to do so. We found out that you can take the SAT more than once, and use the best scores that you get from all the tests. As soon as I found that out, I told them all to get back to studying those SAT books.

"Why not take it again if you can get a better score?" I said. "That first time was just a warm-up."

"That was a hard warm-up, Mrs. Brown," they'd say.

"Life is hard. You got any suggestions about that?" I asked.

And you know how that goes. Quite a few of them did as I suggested, and sure enough, they raised their scores on the second try.

They also had to get letters of recommendation, and that's when their community service came in handy. Sure, some of them had teachers in high school who knew them well enough to write a recommendation letter. But unfortunately, some of my students, like Jorge and Krystal, are quieter, and at a school like Castlemont, the only way you're going to get the attention of those overworked teachers is either to be in their face all the time about a problem or to *be* a problem. It's an unfortunate fact throughout the public school system—the smart, quiet kids can get overlooked.

So that community service came in handy twice: first, because some of the colleges wanted it, and second, because it gave some of the quieter kids a chance to get to know an authority figure well enough to get a recommendation letter. For the kids who asked their teachers to send in recommendations, I told them to double-check with the teachers every week to make sure the letters had been sent. If the college allowed it, I told the kids to pick up the recommendation letter from their teacher and send it in with their applications. That way we could be sure that everything was sent to the school, and sent there on time!

The kids also had to write personal statements. Sometimes the application asked a particular question, like, "What would you say was the most important moment in your life?" Sometimes the school just asked something generic, like, "Describe yourself in three hundred words." I told the kids to treat these personal statements like they would treat a final exam and take them seriously.

"But Mrs. Brown," they said, "these sound like trick questions. Describe yourself in three hundred words? How am I supposed to do that?"

"They may very well be trick questions," I said. "But you know what? They say they're supposed to be personal statements, so just be yourself. Tell them what you want them to know about you—but only the positive stuff, please."

They always laughed when I said that.

Each school asks you for a reading and processing fee, and, depending on whether the school is public or private, it can cost you up to $60. If you're a low-income student, like my babies were, you can get some fee waivers, but even with fee waivers I still had a total of almost two dozen students applying to sixty-some schools. It was a lot of money, but part of that was also because so many of the students were applying to four-year colleges rather than junior colleges. That was another surprise—and a good one.

We were all surprised at the amount of work it took to actually apply to each school. Some of the kids who applied to three or four colleges—and nearly all of my babies applied to at least two—later told me that it was almost like having a part-time job. I felt like I had another part-time job, too, just helping them get everything together and sent out on time.

It was a miracle, but almost everyone got their applications and financial aid forms in during the first semester of their senior year in high school, which left them the opportunity to really kick back and enjoy themselves during the last semester of high school. For the first time, I relaxed a little bit and told them to enjoy themselves—within reason.

"Don't fail out of school or anything," I said at the first meeting after everyone's applications had been mailed in. "And you make sure you remember that your goal is to *graduate* and go on to college, not get involved with any nonsense that's out here running the streets."

"We know, Mrs. Brown," the kids all said. "Aren't you happy? We're almost there!"

"Almost but not yet," I said. I was trying to be stern, but when I heard them say that, I just started laughing with happiness. "We are almost there, aren't we?"

(Please see "Oral Lee Brown's Tip Sheet for College Acceptance" on page 244 for resources to help you apply to college.)

7

Home to Mississippi

Ever since I was old enough to leave, I've been going back to Mississippi. Even after my mother moved out to California I still visited about every ten years or so. I only stayed in Mississippi for a couple of days, and I rarely stayed in Batesville for more than twenty-four hours. I couldn't give you a reason for why I went back, except for the reason that Mississippi is home and I feel connected to it.

These days, I go back to Mississippi every other year. My grandson is studying business administration at Alcorn State University, which is about ninety miles outside of Jackson. Alcorn is the same college that one of my babies, LaTosha, went to for her undergraduate degree, and while she was there I went to see her a couple of times. So in the past few years I've gotten real familiar with Mississippi again.

I don't do too much when I go back there. There's no one for me to visit—all the families that I remember from the Bottom either moved out to California like we did, or they moved somewhere else. So I stay in a motel. And since I've always found it's best to keep a low profile in smaller southern towns, I don't go into all the restaurants and coffee shops where the locals gather. Usually I spend my time driving around, looking for the places I used to visit as a child.

In recent years those places have become harder and harder to find, because Batesville has changed a lot. With the end of the agricultural economy in this country, most small southern towns are struggling, but Batesville has done pretty well. It's much bigger than it was when I was a child. There are no dirt roads anymore, all of them are paved and smooth. The farms are gone and the cotton press is gone, but there's lots of commercial space for the Wal-Mart and the Sizzler and Denny's. There's a Piggly-Wiggly on almost every corner, too. The only thing left over from my childhood is the old sawmill, which I've heard is still accepting employees.

Of course the biggest thing that's changed in Batesville is segregation. Now I can go anywhere I please, and I can be assured when I walk into the Piggly-Wiggly or the movie theater that the white clerk will call me "ma'am" and do whatever it is I need him to do. I know they say the younger generation has grown up less racist than their parents did, and maybe they have. Or maybe they just can't get away with it the way their parents did. Either way, it's kind of funny, because now that I can go into all those places I couldn't go into as a child—the movie theater, which of course now is all sleek and remodeled, or the public bathrooms that used to have the whites-only sign—I really don't want to. Mostly I just ride by and look at them, the way I used to when I was a kid.

Occasionally I'll run into someone who knew my family,

and that's always interesting. These days it's usually someone who knew one of my older brothers or sisters.

"You're one of the Bivins girls, aren't you?" they'll say, and I'll smile.

"That's right," I say, and we get to talking about old times and our families. It makes me a little sad to learn that the black people who chose to stay in Batesville really aren't much better off than they were when I was a child. Maybe they're working for Wal-Mart instead of picking cotton at Mr. Jim's farm, or maybe they've got a job at the sawmill instead of the cotton press, but economically, they're in the same place. I haven't heard of any black-owned businesses in town. So the black people are still working for a business that's owned by a white man, and they're still making just enough each year to break even and have a little extra for Christmas. Usually they spend more than that, and they start the new year off in debt.

That's what I hear from the people I meet in town, the ones who used to know my family. I don't know what they think of me. They always want to know what school I went to and what I did with my life, and if they ask me specific questions, I'll tell them, but I prefer to say, "I've been doing the same thing as you. Just working." You don't want people to think you've gotten snotty because you own your own business or your own house. But it makes me sad to see that we're no better off in Mississippi than we were before the civil rights movement.

The other thing I enjoy doing in Batesville is attending services at Springfield Aces Baptist Church. It's a little white clapboard church that my whole family went to when I was a child. It wasn't until I moved to New York that I gained an understanding of the spiritual meaning of church.

When I moved to New York, I started going to the Church of God and Christ. I would have gone to a Baptist church, but all my friends from school were going to the Church of God and Christ, and I thought I should at least go to a church where I knew someone. It was a very different experience from the Baptist church, because the members were very strict. Women didn't wear pants or lipstick at any time, not just on Sundays. Members said that a woman's knees should always be covered with a skirt.

The preaching was less dramatic than it was in the Baptist church. I missed that flair—I always did like the whooping preachers—but it was at that church that I started really listening to what the preacher was saying. I became very interested in religion when I was a teenager. Hard times make you turn to someone, and since my mother and father weren't there, I turned to God.

Now, when I say that I turned to God, I don't mean that I became a nun or anything like that. I still enjoyed my teenage years, and I have always believed in having some fun along with all my hard work. But it was during my teenage years in New York that I became really acquainted with God and understood that He had a mission for my life. It wasn't until I was in my early forties that I learned what that mission was, but the seeds were planted then.

So now I enjoy going back to my childhood church in Mississippi, because I know why I'm there. (Plus I don't have to sit up close to the pulpit where the preacher can keep an eye on me.) I'm proud to say that I pray, and I pray for lots of

things: I ask God to give me strength, to watch over the health
and happiness of all my babies, both the ones that I gave birth
to and the ones I adopted, and to take care of all those who
can't help themselves.

And when I'm in Mississippi I pray extra hard, because
while I'm there I notice things that I don't always see while I'm
working hard in Oakland. For example, I notice that the levels of inequality between black and white, rich and poor, and
educated and uneducated just continue to get wider. That's not
to say that they're getting better in Oakland. Oakland's surely
not perfect and neither is Detroit or New York City or Al-
abama or anywhere else you want to go in this country. Everywhere you go you're going to see huge differences between the
haves and the have-nots, and that's a line that's almost always
drawn in color.

Maybe I notice it more in Mississippi because I was born
there, and because I remember so clearly how much it hurt me
as a child. Segregation is gone but poor black people there are
still facing huge challenges. The only difference is that now
there are some black people with money, but many of them
aren't at all interested in helping someone else. There's an attitude of "I got mine, so you get yours the best way you can."
The most obvious place you see this attitude is in the rap
songs, but lots of black people in professional positions feel
this way too.

That's the American way, so in some ways I can understand
their feelings, but when you come from an ethnic group that
has always been beaten down in this country, it's a horrible attitude to have. Because I can remember fifty years ago when
black people were not allowed to sit in the train station. I can

remember fifty years ago when black people were not allowed to go to college. And I can remember *five* years ago, during a trip to Mississippi, when I realized through talking to people that every black business in town was financed by a white person. As far as I'm concerned, we weren't free fifty years ago and we're not free now.

Freedom is when I can visit any town in this country, and walk into the black-owned bank, the black-owned grocery store—or, for that matter, the brown-owned bank and the brown-owned grocery store—and know that the money I'm spending is going to help those families get out of poverty for good. Until we can support ourselves with our own money, we're still second-class citizens.

It's no good to claim that just because you've managed to be successful, everyone else can find their own way. It's great to make some money for yourself and take care of your family. In fact, you have to do that first—you can't pull anyone up if you don't have your own bootstraps. But it's a mistake to think that it ends there. If you're the only one who's free, you're living in a make-believe world. And you're not even living, you're just surviving.

Living is when you stop thinking about yourself and start thinking about the responsibility you have to the people who helped you become successful. If you're black, I don't care how talented you are or how well you've done for yourself— you're standing on the shoulders of the civil rights movement. Therefore, those of us who have made it have a responsibility to all those people who were getting beaten up at lunch counters, all those people who were sprayed across the street by fire hoses, all those people who went to jail because they refused to go to the back of the bus, and we definitely have a responsibility to people like James Meredith, who made great personal sacrifices to desegregate the University of Mississippi. Those people made it possible for the rest of us to get the education you have to have in order to be successful in this country.

So that's what I think about whenever I go back to Mississippi. I think about how far I've come, and how far many of the people around me have *not* come. I think about how I'd really like to see others like me, who have made it, decide that they're not going to get a new car for a few years. Instead, they're going to take that money and see how they can use it to help someone else get an education. I'm not necessarily talking about helping a cousin or a brother or a niece, either—that's family, and it's great to help family, but that's no way to fulfill the larger responsibility we have to the people who made it possible for us.

That's how I feel about the matter. I can't imagine how any person of color who's managed to move to the other side of town could travel to Mississippi—or East Oakland, for that matter—and fail to recognize an obligation to make things better for the people there, preferably through something lasting like an education. But whenever I make this argument to someone, this is the response I often hear: "But I can't find anyone to help, Mrs. Brown," they say. "A lot of these kids don't have the motivation to make something of themselves."

"Those are exactly the ones you need to help," I say. "Find the worst kid on the block. Find the kid who's been picked up for truancy. Find the kid whose parents have given up on him. Find the kid you really can't stand because he's got such a bad attitude. Sit him down and talk to him. Ask him why he doesn't want to go to school. Ask him if he's thought about going to college. Tell him you want to walk out on faith and see if you can help him make a difference in his life with education. And see what he has to say. I bet you'll be surprised."

I'm convinced that most of these so-called bad kids out there would blossom after a conversation like that. I think those conversations need to happen everywhere in this country, although obviously the need is even greater in places like Batesville, where black people haven't been free to better themselves for as long as they have in Oakland.

Several years ago, my two daughters and I went on a family trip to Mississippi. We didn't stay very long. My girls don't like Mississippi much either. They never liked visiting when they were kids, and they certainly don't like it now that they're adults. It's hot, the mosquitoes bother them, and they don't know what to think of the way people live there.

"Why do black people keep living in places like Mississippi?" one of my daughters asked me.

"I don't know," I said. "Obviously they like it or they wouldn't still be here."

"Well, I'm glad that I didn't have to live here," she said.

"I know, baby, I made sure that you didn't," I said. "That's why I've always worked so hard."

I meant that. I am very glad that my children didn't have to grow up in Mississippi, and whenever I go back I'm amazed at how far I've come since my childhood. According to what I learned in Batesville, black people weren't supposed to do what I've done. I haven't forgotten that lesson, the lesson that black people are not supposed to be successful. Because I know that quite a few people, in Batesville and otherwise, still believe it's true, because they can't see a way out of poverty. As long as that's true for them, it'll be true for me, and that's why I've worked so hard with my daughters and my babies in Oakland. I'm trying to teach all of us new lessons, one person at a time.

8

Graduation

I felt like their senior year in high school just sailed by. It seemed like we'd barely pulled out those first SAT practice tests before the girls were dragging me out to shop for their prom dresses. I remember shopping for prom dresses particularly well because it took *forever.* Those girls tore apart every dress store in Bayfair Mall looking for their gowns. I tried to keep up with them, but eventually I just had to find a bench and sit down.

"Come find me when you know what you want," I told the girls when we walked into the mall for the third or fourth time.

"But Mrs. Brown, you've got to come with us," they'd say.

"I'm tired," I told them. "Besides, I don't have anything to say about these fashions you young girls are wearing these days. Some of these dresses, I can't believe they let you in the door with them on."

"Aww, Mrs. Brown, you're missing half the fun," they said, rushing into the next store.

"There's enough fun out here," I said, mostly to myself. I

was more than happy to sit outside while they shopped, and I spent the time wondering how everything had gone by so fast.

The prom and all the senior class activities were fantastic. We've got so many pictures of the girls in their pretty gowns, the boys in their sharp tuxedos, everybody preening and posing for the camera. A lot of the students at Castlemont and Skyline chipped in and rented limousines for the evening, but I told my babies if they wanted to do that they'd have to pay for it themselves.

"Seventeen years old and riding around in a limousine?" I said. "When I was seventeen years old I thought the best thing in the world was a taxi ride."

"Yeah, yeah, yeah, Mrs. Brown," the kids laughed. But to their credit, I think my babies understand financial responsibility a lot better than some of their peers in East Oakland. I certainly tried to teach them.

"Don't go out buying a fancy car before you own your own house," I told them. "You can make money on a house, but you're only going to lose on a car. And don't be one of these folks out here on the street—I know you know who I'm talking about—buying a $200 pair of Nikes, on credit, and doesn't have a penny in the bank."

They rolled their eyes at my preaching, but they got the point. So far, all my babies who have graduated from college have done so without any credit card debt—at least to my knowledge.

The kids' college acceptance letters started rolling in while they were getting ready for their senior proms. Those letters were even more exciting for the kids than their prom. The senior prom was about saying good-bye to their high schools and all their friends. It made high school graduation seem real. But the acceptance letters reminded them that they had better things ahead of them. All of a sudden, it wasn't me standing above them telling them that they could make it into college; they had a letter in their hands that said they *had* made it into college—or they had acceptance letters from two colleges, or three.

Many of my students were accepted to multiple colleges, a fact that makes me very proud. We got acceptance letters from some of the best colleges in the state and the country— Howard University, the University of California at Berkeley, the University of California at Davis, not to mention lots of the California State Universities. I'm not the type of person who carries grudges, but I have to admit that I did gloat a little bit when my babies started hearing from colleges. All those offers to go to college for kids who people told me would never go anywhere!

Some of the kids who received multiple acceptances had a stressful experience picking a single college, but I said they had better be happy about their situations.

"It's much better than not having any choice at all," I told them when they came to me with a handful of letters and a long face.

"But I'm not sure how to pick," they said. "All of them have something that I want."

From the beginning of high school, I told my babies that I was not going to pick a college for them. I didn't even want to offer advice, and I'll tell you why. I didn't have to go to college, they did. I didn't have to take exams. I didn't have to write papers. I didn't have to deal with roommates who might or might not have sense. I wanted them to make their own decision and take responsibility for it, because I did not want to ever hear someone complaining about how they had gone to a college that I wanted them to go to and they didn't like it.

"No college is going to be perfect," I told them. "So you make your own decision and you live with the consequences."

Now, if I had my way, they all would have been at black colleges. But I knew that voicing my opinion would be unfair, because I wasn't the one who had to go. I wanted them to go where they felt comfortable and where they would be happy, so if they came to me looking for advice about where to go I would not give it to them.

"I can't tell you what to do, because I'm not you," I said. "Why don't you make a chart for each college and put all the negatives on one side and the positives on the other. Compare them and see what you get."

And I did this with many of my babies when they came into my real estate office, sniffling about how confused they were. I'd sit the student—let's call her Elizabeth—down at a desk with a couple pieces of paper and a pen, and tell her to write down what she did and didn't like.

"Okay, Mrs. Brown," Elizabeth said, and as she made her charts she'd call out what she liked and didn't like.

"I like that it's got a good business department," she said, as I calmly went about my business with a real estate listing.

"Umm-hmm," I said.

"But I don't like that it's far away," she said. "And I think it's cold there, too—what do you think, Mrs. Brown?"

"I really don't know, Elizabeth," I said. "Go on with the next college, now."

The only advice I did give them was to focus on what a college had to offer, not how much it cost. The foundation paid for whatever the college's financial aid—in the form of grants—wouldn't cover. I didn't want my babies to graduate with student loans, like most students do these days. I think that's unfair, and it pushes a lot of kids into jobs for which they don't feel any passion. That happens to most poor people in this country, and for once I wanted my babies starting off on an equal footing with the more privileged people they'd meet. When they graduated, I didn't want them deferring their dreams because of college debt.

Debt, unfortunately, is one of the nasty little secrets no one ever told me about when I started helping my kids apply for college. I was shocked at the stingy financial aid plans my babies were offered from the colleges that accepted them. I was even more shocked when I found out later that they got some of the most generous plans out there!

I'll just give you an example: let's say one of my students got accepted into a school that cost $14,000 a year in tuition, room, and board. That college would offer what they called a plan for low-income students: grants of $6,000 a year and loans of $4,000 a year. That still leaves $4,000 a year for the student to pay, and they call that a plan for low-income students?

When I asked about this, I found out that colleges figure out their financial aid plans by looking at the income of a student's parents. A lot of colleges seem to believe that if a child's parents are making $20,000 a year, they can devote thousands of dollars per year toward that child's college tuition, and that's *on top* of the loans the student is expected to take on.

I'm not sure who that kind of plan works for, but it certainly wouldn't have worked for my babies. For one thing, a lot of my students' parents weren't putting a dime toward their children's education. If not for the Oral Lee Brown Foundation, all my students would have had to come up with the difference between what the financial aid office said they could pay and what they actually had—sometimes a difference of $6,000 to $8,000 a year. If I were a poor eighteen-year-old student trying to go to college, I'd stop right there. I'd think the college acceptance board was playing a joke on me. Once again, my students were lucky. I'd been saving their college tuition for years. Even though it wasn't as much money as I would've liked to save for them, it was still enough so that they didn't have to consider cost when they were making their decision about where to go to college. But it hurt me to see those financial aid offers, because I know how many poor children who are out there who couldn't possibly make the sort of "financial contributions" that most colleges expect. As the cost of college goes up, things are only going to get worse.

If you're a low-income parent, I've said it once and I'll say it again: start saving for your child's college education *as soon as you can.* Preferably at birth, but if not then, at least by the time your child enters kindergarten. If you don't have a lot of money, you can't expect any help from these institutions that claim they will make it affordable for your child to go to college, so start thinking about your savings for their tuition the same way you'd think about your rent, your food bills, your electricity. You may have to do without cable television or the Internet, but that's not asking a lot, considering what you'll get for your sacrifice.

It becomes even more important to stay on top of your child's grades, too. If you don't have a lot of money to send your child to college, grades are even more crucial. With good grades your child can get the scholarships that might make up that $5,000- to $6,000-a-year shortfall. If the scholarships aren't coming from the college your child wants to attend, there are many available from outside sources—professional associations, Rotary clubs, churches. I've included some resources for finding outside scholarships at the end of this book.

❧

I wish to this day that we'd had the time and the energy to look into getting outside scholarships for my babies. We were so busy just making sure that everyone was keeping their grades up, taking their SAT tests, and getting their applications in on time that we didn't have a chance to do the research—and it is a lot of research. But I don't wish that we'd gotten outside scholarships because I'd rather not have spent my own money. I'd pay for their college education two or three times over if I had to. It just bothers me that a lot of those scholarships go to kids who can already afford college, simply because poor students don't know where to look for them. Plus, it would have been an additional boost for my babies' self-esteem. It's always nice when someone rewards you for doing a good job.

Quite a few of the outside scholarships are really generous; some associations even offer full rides for the brightest kids. A full scholarship still comes with hidden fees, though. As soon as my babies went to college we learned about costs that weren't mentioned in their assessments for financial aid. There are campus fees for sports and clubs; books, which can cost thousands of dollars a year; and new clothes, especially for kids who are going to a college in a part of the country with a different climate from home. If I tried to add up all the unexpected costs from that first year alone, it would make my head spin. The bottom line is that if you're poor, no one's going to help you. So you'll just have to keep that in mind, and plan accordingly.

By the time the kids had decided where they wanted to go to school, they were getting brochures in school about class rings and graduation gown fittings. The kids were beside themselves with excitement, but they were also a little sad. Lots of their friends from school weren't graduating with them. Some had dropped out earlier and were working dead-end jobs, and some hadn't passed classes and would be graduating later. I told them not to be sad.

"You should be all the more proud of what you've accomplished," I told them. "It's not easy to succeed when all around you, you've got people who are doing the opposite."

They were proud. They shrugged it off in front of some of their friends who weren't graduating, but they were thrilled with the fact that they had made it. Not as thrilled as I was, though. All these years. All these years struggling with poverty and hard work and people's cynical expectations, and we'd done it. We'd proven everyone wrong.

If possible, I was even more excited about the graduations than they were. For a minute, I wished that all of them were at the same high school, so we could get "Oral Lee Brown class" pictures and they could all throw their hats up at the same moment. But my babies were graduating from six different high schools. Most of them were at Castlemont; four of them were at Skyline; the rest were scattered in other East Oakland high schools and a few outside of Oakland. And eventually I realized that six graduations meant six different opportunities for me to be as proud as punch.

I went to all of them. I wore my best clothes. I brought my camera and took lots of pictures. When their names were announced, I didn't stand up and yell like I thought I might. I was so choked up I couldn't even get up. I stayed in my seat, and I clapped until my hands hurt.

When the ceremony was over, I took pictures of the students—or student, if there was only one. Very few of the students' parents showed up to the high school graduations, but the kids didn't seem to mind, and for once, I didn't either. The students knew what they had done; they were dancing with happiness. In fact, some of them asked why I was so quiet.

"Aren't you happy, Mrs. Brown?" they said. "If I were you I'd be jumping for the sky right about now."

"You guys have already done that," I said.

I still have the programs from those graduations. I don't keep any of the plaques that people give me for establishing this foundation; I don't know what the foundation board has done with all the letters of congratulations we've gotten over the years. But I know where the programs for my babies' graduations are.

Six graduations also meant six media opportunities, although the media was the furthest thing from my mind. The foundation started hearing from different media outlets a few weeks before the kids graduated. Of course the local newspapers and television stations called, but we were also getting calls from the majors: ABC, NBC, CBS, CNN, the *New York Times*, the *Chicago Tribune*. I knew that something was going on when we got a call from someone at Oprah's show. Now *that* knocked me off my feet.

"Where did all these people get this phone number from?" I asked the foundation board. "How'd they find out what's going on here?"

No one had any answers for me. I've since found out that the local media keeps clip files of events, so reporters probably found the articles that were written in 1987 and decided it was time to find out if I had, indeed, kept my promise. But I don't have a clue as to how the national media found out about my students.

I didn't complain about it, even though the media has always made me nervous. I don't like the attention. Besides, I didn't do anything special — I just helped these kids get a better chance in life. That wouldn't be special if everyone else would do it, too. I did a couple of interviews, and then for the most part I ignored the phone. I created a message on the answering machine that offered the dates and times of the graduations, as well as the phone number for each school principal. I figured if the media was interested in the story, they could go to the graduations and talk to the kids — I simply didn't see why all these newspapers and television programs wanted to talk to me.

Still, my foundation board urged me to do interviews. "It'll be good for the foundation, Mrs. Brown," they said, and they were right. Every time we went on a major television program, like the *Today* show or *Dateline*, donations poured in. I realized that we made an average of about $20,000 every time I made a television appearance, and I relented — a little bit.

"I'm only going to go on programs that have shown respect for education," I said. So I went on the *Today* show, because Katie Couric has always shown so much enthusiasm for public education projects. I'm glad that I did — Katie Couric didn't disappoint. She was warm and personable, and she went out of her way to make sure that Jeffery and Nekita, who were on the show with me, felt comfortable. She also went above and beyond the call of duty by asking each of her viewers to send in a dollar. Not all of them did as they were told—we got about $32,000 in donations after that program—but I was impressed with her dedication.

Katie Couric also called me her hero, which shocked me. I've never thought I could be anyone's hero. I'm just doing what the Lord asked me to do.

I had other interesting experiences with the media, too. Peter Jennings wanted to do a show about our success, so his staff arranged to attend LaTosha Hunter's graduation. You can imagine the uproar all those cameras caused; a poor black school in East Oakland having a simple graduation and all of a sudden, Peter Jennings's staff shows up! We had lots of fun, though. Later on when I met him he seemed like such a serious man, but he showed a lot of warmth toward the kids and really made an effort to understand what they were up against. Tom Brokaw missed the graduations, but he asked if he could come by when the kids came home from college for their first Christmas. The kids were amazed about that—they came into the foundation expecting one of our usual gatherings, and there was Tom Brokaw and a million cameras.

I also went on *Oprah*, because she's Oprah. She was great. She was touched by the idea of a regular woman like me dedicating so much of my time and money to help kids get to college, and she issued a challenge to her viewers to create the same sort of foundation in their own communities. I really appreciated that, because if anything, that's why I'd like people to pay attention to us—not because we did something so special here, but because we can serve as an example to people who want to do the same thing.

Fielding the media requests was part of the graduation, but for the most part, I was focused on getting my babies off to college. In a lot of ways the experience of sending them off to college was as exhausting as the application process. There were so many things they needed . . . for example, after they'd decided which college they wanted to go to, the kids got packets of information about their housing and orientation programs. They also got letters from the school that encouraged them to bring certain things with them. Almost all of the colleges "strongly encouraged" them to bring a personal computer with them. I'd learned that whenever a school claims to "strongly encourage" something, it's practically mandatory.

Now, maybe for the middle-class kids who make up most of the college population, buying an $800 personal computer is no big deal. But obviously that was not going to be the case for me and my students—they couldn't even imagine coming up with the money for a personal computer, even a used one, and I certainly didn't have the resources to help all of them. I started worrying about computers as soon as the students got those letters in April—my babies, bless their hearts, weren't even worried about where the computers were going to come from—and I worried about it all the way through graduation.

Like I've always said, though, God will send you what you need if you pray hard enough. What I needed came in the form of a telephone call from the donations office at the University of California at Berkeley. UC Berkeley has been aware of the Oral Lee Brown Foundation since the mid-1990s, ever since

Janessa Joffey recruited some students to help tutor the kids. Plus, one of my students, Jorge, was accepted to UC Berkeley, and I had had a long talk with the financial aid office about our program and the sorts of financial difficulties my students were facing. So maybe it was through these things, or maybe it was just through the hand of God, that they decided to call me with a suggestion the summer before my babies went off to college.

"Mrs. Brown, we're updating some of the computers in our undergraduate division," said the official at the donations office. "And someone over here remembered your foundation."

"You were working with this foundation before we were famous," I said with a laugh. "And we do appreciate that."

"Well, I'm glad to hear that we've been doing something right over here," he said. "We'd be happy to do more, if you think you have a use for some old computers."

"As a matter of fact, we do," I said. "How many do you have?"

"How many do you need?" he said.

"You just became my favorite person of the day," I said.

That's how we got the computers. The donations office even sent a few students over to the foundation to help install software and show the kids how to assemble their computers once they got into their dorms. With that hurdle overcome, I set out to attack the next one: getting the kids packed up and ready to start their new lives.

For the kids who were moving across the country, moving all their things—not to mention their hopes—was a huge undertaking. There was no way we could carry everything they needed with them on the airplane, so we shipped a lot of their things to the dorm address they'd gotten with their orientation packets and hoped for the best.

"But Mrs. Brown, what if it doesn't get there?" said many of my teary-eyed students, as they watched their hard-earned possessions creep down the conveyer belt at the post office.

"I wouldn't worry about it too much," I said calmly, craning my own neck to watch the boxes slip away. "But all the same, when you get home, you might want to just let God know that you'd like your things back." I flew out with all the students who were going to colleges far away, and of course no one lost anything.

For the kids who were attending a college within driving distance, we packed everything they needed into the back of my car. Then we drove down the highway with the back of the car sagging and the student acting as navigator through the traffic that I couldn't see out of my back window!

When I look back on it now, it was a lot of fun, although of course at the time it was pretty stressful. We received an anonymous donation from a couple who stipulated that we give $1,000 to each child who was going to college, to buy books and clothes and items for their dorm rooms. So as soon as we'd gotten to the college campus and I'd helped each student unpack his or her boxes, we went shopping for whatever he or she still needed.

That experience was very funny, because my students shop the way they act, if you know what I mean. For example, one of the things I've always admired about Nekita Noel is that she's very careful with her money, and she's not materialistic at all. She never wanted new Nikes or anything like that. As long as she was clean and none of her clothes had holes in them, she was happy. So I've always admired that about her, but I—that would be me, Oral Lee Brown, who shopped at Payless Shoe Source for twenty years—I had to let her know on her college shopping trip that she could go too far with that frugal attitude. We went to buy new clothes, and the girl wanted to go to the cheapest store in town. Then, when we got there, she wanted to buy the cheapest clothes in the store.

"Nekita," I told her, "these clothes are going to fall apart the first time you put them in the washing machine. Can't you maybe get the sweater that's got a little wool in it, the one that costs ten dollars instead of five?"

"I will, Mrs. Brown, I just want to make sure my money goes as far as it can go," she said.

"That's great, Nekita, but it's going to be gone real fast if you have to buy new clothes every month," I said.

So we got to make some fun memories, too. And I have to say this—I wasn't sad when it was time to say good-bye. If you're wondering whether or not I have a heart, believe me, it wasn't because I was ready to be rid of my babies. I already missed them terribly, and it only got worse as the months went on. But when it came to leaving them on a college campus with everything they needed to be successful—materially *and* spiritually—I just felt good.

But my babies didn't. They all got sad when I started to leave, and quite a few of them cried. When that happened, I sat the student down on a bench and started talking.

"Why are you crying?" I said. "Why do you think you've been going to school all these years? Why do you think you stayed up all night finishing those school reports? Why do you think you fought through that SAT? Why do you think you went through all that math tutoring? This is what it was for."

"I'm scared, Mrs. Brown," they said. "And I'm going to miss you."

"You can just hush up about being scared," I said. "You've

got nothing to be scared about. You've done it. You made it! You should be happy right now. Don't worry about missing me. I'm not going anywhere. So give me a kiss and dry your eyes."

Eventually they would stop sniffling, and then we'd walk back to their dorm and meet their roommates. They started talking to the kids they'd be going to school with and pretty soon, they would smile again. I didn't leave any of my students crying. I always waited until they were over the pain of separation, after they remembered how excited they were about what lay ahead.

"You've got my phone number if you ever want to call," I said as I left. "And I do hope you will call."

"Of course I will, Mrs. Brown," came the reply, and all the students did call. In fact, they called me more during that first year of college than they had in high school. They told me about everything that was going on in college, everything they liked and disliked. So I never had to worry about empty-nest syndrome. I felt like my babies were still with me, just a little bit farther away.

∾

One of them is still with me in spirit, even though she's much farther away than the others. Just when my babies were getting settled into their new lives at college, just when we were all starting to relax with the knowledge that we had beaten the odds, tragedy struck. We lost Tracy Easterling in the fall of 2002.

If the Oral Lee Brown Foundation had a poster child, Tracy would be it. She was born with every possible strike against her and she responded with a loud, proud attitude. She was a smart student—far smarter than most of her teachers ever gave her credit for. She loved all of her brothers and sisters in the program—I've got her to thank for bringing Jeffery back into the fold. We all loved her even when she was driving us crazy, and I don't think any of us will ever get over her death.

What made it even harder was the way she died. Tracy was just entering her sophomore year at Laney College in Oakland, where she was studying cosmetology. She had a difficult family situation, which is one of the reasons she decided to go to school close to home. She wanted to make sure she was close in case anything happened.

I was working at my real estate office one Saturday morning in November when I got a phone call from Tracy. She was spending the weekend at home with her family, but she wanted to know what I was doing.

"I need to talk to you," she said.

"You dialed the number, you know where I am," I said. "When do you want to come by?"

"How long are you going to be there?" she asked.

"I'll be here until around two-thirty," I said. "Then I have to run over to Bayfair Mall and pick up a few things. I'm going to New York tomorrow." I was going to do some media interviews for the foundation.

"Okay," she said. "I'll come by before then."

I waited for her until two-thirty, and then I left for the mall. When I got back to my office, it was almost four o'clock. My plane for New York left at five-thirty. I checked my watch and asked Helen, my secretary, if Tracy had come by.

"No, she didn't," Helen said.

"Did she call?" I asked.

"Nope," Helen said.

I looked at my watch again. I'm nervous when it comes to flying on airplanes, and I was already worried about missing this one. I knew that a conversation with Tracy—or with any of my babies for that matter—could take an awfully long time. Still, I had a funny feeling about the conversation we'd had a few hours before.

"Did she sound upset when you talked to her?" Helen asked.

"No, not at all," I said.

"It's probably not a big deal, then," she said.

"You're right, it's probably not," I said. "All the same, why don't you put down on my schedule that I need to call her as soon as I get back."

"All right," Helen said, and I went on to the airport.

I hadn't been in New York for one full day before I got a message at my hotel that Helen had called—and it was urgent.

"She didn't leave a message?" I asked the woman at the front desk.

"No, ma'am, she didn't," she said. "She just said that you need to call her back immediately."

I just stood there, looking at the message. I had the same feeling I had the night Willie Bea called me about my daughter Michelle. I was afraid to call Helen back and afraid not to call her back. I might have stood there in front of the front desk at that hotel for hours if the clerk hadn't spoken to me again.

"Ma'am," she said, "are you all right?"

I snapped my head up to look at her. She stared at me with concern, waiting for an answer, but I didn't give her one—instead I tore my eyes away and ran for the elevator. As soon as

I was back in my room I grabbed the phone and dialed my office number.

"Helen," I said, "what's going on?"

She was quiet for a long minute, and I said, "You better start talking, Helen. What's happening over there?"

"I think you need to come home, Mrs. Brown," she said. "Tracy's been shot."

"Oh my God . . ."

"She's okay, they say she's okay, Mrs. Brown," Helen said, but I wasn't listening. I knew she wasn't telling me the truth.

"Helen," I interrupted, "I'm calling downstairs right now and I'll be at the airport in less than an hour. I'm going to call you from the airport as soon as I get a plane—can you stay at the office until then?"

"I sure can," she said, and I hung up the phone with her and made two phone calls—one to the airline I was traveling on, and one to the woman at the front desk. The airline agreed to change my ticket, and the woman at the front desk called a car to take me to the airport—a limousine, no less. Like I was headed out to my prom night. The whole experience felt all the more crazy to me because I was driving to the airport in a limousine while one of my babies was lying in a hospital.

I caught the first plane flying back to the Bay Area, so all in all it was about two hours between the time I got Helen's message and the time I got on the plane. Just before I boarded, I called Helen again.

"Have you heard from the hospital?" I asked.

"I just talked to them," Helen said. "They say she's okay, but you should still get over here."

"Is that what they said, Helen?"

"That's what they said, Mrs. Brown."

I was silent on the other end of the phone.

"Mrs. Brown? Are you there?"

"I have to go, Helen," I said quietly. "My plane's boarding."

"Okay, Mrs. Brown, someone will be there to pick you up at the airport," she said, and I hung up the phone.

That was a long, restless flight. I'm agitated on flights anyway, but this time it wasn't due to nervousness. This time it was due to something else, and it got so bad that halfway through the flight I just burst into tears.

"What's wrong?" asked the woman sitting next to me, whose name was Jeanette.

And I just kept right on crying. For whatever reason, it was hard to carry the burden alone that night, and I wasn't even embarrassed to let this strange woman know it. "Why do people lie to me?" I replied, and not so much to answer her question as to answer my own. "I know that Tracy's not okay."

"Is that what they're telling you?" she asked kindly, and eventually the whole story came out—to this woman sitting next to me on the flight. I'm not sure what came over me, to tell her everything like that, but it must have helped. By the time the plane landed, my eyes were dry. I felt calm and terrified, which is, I've learned, a good way to feel in a crisis situation. If things were as bad as I was afraid they were, I didn't want to be a mess going into that hospital. Tracy's family would need me to be strong.

An old friend of mine picked me up from the airport. He asked me if I wanted to go directly to the hospital, and at first I said yes. A few minutes later, I changed my mind.

"Take me home," I said. "Don't take me to that hospital just yet." That familiar feeling was coming back—the feeling I had the night that Michelle died, and the feeling I had that night when my daughter called me about the armed robbery at my restaurant, Cobblers. I didn't want to go to the hospital because I didn't know what I was going to find there.

"Whatever you say," he said, and he turned the car around and took me home. He carried my bag into my house and told me to call him when I found out what was going on.

"Any time of the day or night, you hear?" he said.

"Thanks, baby," I said, knowing full well that I needed to find out what was going on right then. And that's what I did — as soon as I walked into my house I fumbled in the dark for the phone and called Highland Hospital.

When I called, at first I had to deal with all the stupid bureaucracy that you have to go through when you call a hospital — touch-tone menus, being put on hold, all of it. I thought my teeth were going to crumble from gritting them so hard. When I finally got through to an attendant, I first asked her to check the status of a patient, and then I changed my mind.

"Put me through to Tracy Easterling's room," I said.

"Well, you know, miss, we only allow relatives to speak to patients in the rooms —"

"I *am* a relative," I yelled. "And she won't even be able to speak. So put me through. Ask for Eloise."

Eloise is Tracy's grandmother. She was Tracy's second mother, since Tracy's parents weren't able to provide for her. She was one of the reasons why Tracy loved the program so much, because Eloise understood what I was trying to do and always made herself available to help. She and I became very close on a personal level as well, and I knew that if something was wrong with Tracy, she would be there.

"Eloise," I said when she got on the phone, "what's going on over there?"

"Are you back home, Mrs. Brown?" she asked. "Are you in Oakland?"

"I just got back," I said.

"Where are you right now?"

"I'm at home," I said.

"You need to come out here, Mrs. Brown," Eloise said.

When she said that, I closed my eyes and gripped the doorknob of my front door—I was still standing in the front entry of my house, in the dark. I gripped the doorknob because I wanted to stay on my feet.

"You there, Mrs. Brown?" Eloise said.

"I'm here," I said. "I'm here, Eloise."

"She's still holding on right now," Eloise went on. "But that's because we've asked the hospital to keep her breathing. We didn't want them to take her off until you got here."

I gripped the doorknob harder.

"She was dead as soon as they shot her," she said.

"Who shot her, Eloise?"

Silence on the other end of the phone.

"*Who* shot her, Eloise?"

"I don't know, Mrs. Brown."

I don't remember much of what happened between that conversation and my arrival at the hospital. In fact, I don't remember much of what happened between my arrival at the hospital and Tracy's funeral a few days later. I must have driven myself to the hospital, or gotten a friend to drive me. I got there somehow.

Once I was there, I must have talked to the staff at the hospital, talked to Tracy's family, maybe I even talked to Tracy as she lay there in the bed. She wouldn't have been able to respond to me. She had two bullets in her head and one in her neck. There was nothing that I could have said that would have been able to reach her.

That's not my typical response to death. I remember everything that happened surrounding Michelle's death, at least everything that happened while I was awake. I remember running around making arrangements after EQ's death, even though I was devastated. And of course I remember everything that went into preparing my grandmother and my father after they died. But I don't remember anything that happened between Tracy's death and the funeral, and I think that's because I felt so much regret that I didn't call Tracy back that day.

I know I couldn't have prevented her death. At some point later when I felt a little more steady on my feet I went down to the police station to find out everything that they knew about what had happened. Captain Richard Word, who is now the chief of police, was the first to arrive at the scene. He told me that Tracy's family had been having a barbecue in their backyard. They had all been making a greater effort to get along, and they thought they'd do something as a family. Tracy, who must have been delighted about the barbecue, offered to walk to the store and pick up some lighter fluid. She was walking down the street on her way to the corner store.

As she turned on 94th Avenue, she walked past a young man. This young man had been involved in some kind of fight with a group of other young men—I don't know if it was a gang fight or what. What I do know is that this group of young men he was fighting with drove by in a car at the very moment he was walking past Tracy, and he grabbed her by the waist and held her in front of him as they drove past. They sprayed her with bullets and drove off. The man who had used her as a shield dropped her on the street and then ran off himself. The police department couldn't find any of those men then and they still haven't found them.

"What do you mean you've got no suspects!" I yelled at Captain Word—and his superiors, too. I was ready to take on the whole Oakland Police Department. East Oakland's not huge; they must have known who was fighting with whom. How could they be so useless?

I had to remind myself to calm down, that whatever their faults, the Oakland Police Department had not killed Tracy. On the other hand, going down there to ask if anything had been done about her death only made me upset, so I stopped going down there, too. I acknowledged the fact that when a poor person, especially a poor black person, is murdered in this country, most police departments aren't going to put all that much effort into finding out who did it. I focused my attention on what *I* could do—and that meant spending time with Tracy's family, making arrangements for the burial, and calling all of her brothers and sisters in the program to let them know what had happened.

All of them were devastated. Later, Jeffery said, "That was my friend. I had a lot of love for Tracy, crazy as she was. When she died it really opened my eyes, and helped me see that even if you have all the blessings in the world, the devil can take them away, just that quick. She shouldn't have been anywhere near East Oakland. She was a smart girl, she was going to college, and she knew this place would've destroyed her. But she wanted to take care of her family, and that was the price, I guess. I was so angry about that for a long time. It made me all the more determined to stay out of East Oakland, because I knew that there was nothing there for any of us."

All of the students who were living in the area came back for her funeral. For the ones who were far away, I spent lots of time with them on the phone talking about what had happened. Some of them wanted to cry with me about it, and we cried together. Some of them just wanted to talk about her, and share their memories of her, and I listened. A lot of them called each other and talked about her, and that made me feel really good. They proved that they could stick together in a crisis, like a real family.

I tried not to tell any of my students how I was really feeling, even though many of them asked. I always told them I was getting by, which was the truth, but I was also full of sadness and regret. The fact that I didn't call Tracy back that day when she was going to come see me bothered me more than anything has ever bothered me in my life. She wanted to talk to me about something. I don't know what she wanted to say, and now I'll never know. Maybe she had a little thought in the back of her head that she needed to share with me on what turned out to be the last day of her life. She never got the chance to do so, because I didn't give her that chance. I had the opportunity to call her back, and I didn't. You have to live with some things. And I have to live with that.

9

A New Class

I still haven't gotten over the loss of Tracy. I don't think I ever will. It's no accident that I decided to take on a new class of students shortly after her death. I won't say that I was trying to make up for the fact that I wasn't able to save her, but I will say that her death made me feel the needs of the children in my community even more. After I lost one of my own who never got the chance to live up to her potential, I became that much more aware of the kids around me who were desperately hoping for an education. I had experience with helping those kids, so I couldn't see any reason for not stepping in to help.

Besides, the foundation was getting so many phone calls. Every time I made an appearance on television, a flood of sad messages from kids all over the country would pour in. It got to the point that I asked Helen, my secretary, to go into the office half an hour earlier in the morning, just to clear out all the messages on the answering machine. I certainly couldn't listen to them. Some of them were from parents, who would always ask, very politely, if maybe I would consider paying for their kids to go to college.

But I was amazed by how many of the requests came from children. Most of them were in high school, but more than a few were still in junior high school. They all told the same familiar story to the answering machine, or to Helen when she was there to pick up the phone:

"Mrs. Brown, I saw you on TV and I was just wondering if there was any way for you to *puh-leeze* accept me as one of your Oral B. kids. I really want to go to college and there's no way my parents can pay for me to go. I've kept my grades up, just like you said I should do on TV. So please call me back and let me know if I can be in the program too. I promise I'll be really nice to all the other Oral B. kids."

And poor Helen had to tell all those desperate kids that no, the foundation wasn't set up to accept any more students, but that she wished them the best.

"I just feel so awful telling them no, Mrs. Brown," she told me one day after she had been telling them *no* nonstop for at least six months. "They don't really argue with me, but they get so sad. They say, 'Well, now how am I going to get to college?' And I just tell them they should apply for scholarships. But most of them don't even know where to go for those."

"I know," I said. "It makes me so mad. They shouldn't have to call and beg like that."

Eventually it made me mad enough that I decided that maybe I should step up to the plate and do something about it. I've always said that you shouldn't get mad about the things you can change—you should just change them and stop complaining. And although I'd learned by now that my brother

EQ was right—in fact I *can't* change the whole world—at least I can change the little corner that I'm living in.

So in 2001, I found myself going before my foundation's board to ask how they would feel about taking on a new class of students.

"I know I'm asking you to do more than you signed up for," I said. "I'm asking you to do a lot more than you signed up for. For that matter I'm asking *myself* to do more than I signed up for."

"Well, don't make it sound so enticing, Oral," said Julie, one of my board members.

I laughed. "Well, I think you all know that the need for the kind of work that we're doing is huge. You've all heard the phone calls we've been getting from kids who are trying to find a way to go to college."

Everyone nodded.

"I think that we have a real opportunity here to fill some of that need. Especially since we know what we're doing. What do you say?"

There was silence.

"Oh, come on now. I certainly don't need this. I'm about to retire. I own my house. I own my car. I could be all set to sail off into the Caribbean, if that's what I wanted to do. The Lord knows I've done my part for these kids."

Now the board members laughed.

I took a look at my board members and smiled. We really have been through so much together. Many of them started out as my personal friends and we've grown closer through the foundation, and the rest of us have become friends through our work with the kids. One of my first board members, Julie

Toliver, didn't know anything about community service when she signed up to help—just like me. I met Julie through a local real estate association, and when I told her, tentatively, about the adoption, she didn't laugh at me like everyone else did. Instead she told me immediately that she would help. That's what I call a good friend.

Julie liked working with the foundation, and she told her friends about it. Some of them joined us on the board, and they told *their* friends, which is how I was fortunate enough to find great folks like Mr. Mitchell. I had intended the board to be very small, because I didn't think they'd be doing much, but I should have expected more from the great people who work with me.

Even the newest board members—David Osborne and his wife, Georgia Osborne—have done a tremendous amount for me and the kids. The Osbornes are far more affluent than the rest of the board members are—they're far more affluent than I am, too—but they don't put on any airs at all. They're just as sweet as they can be. Mr. Osborne first heard about the foundation when he saw Tom Brokaw's news special on the work that I had done with the first class of students. It stuck in the back of his mind for months. Soon he was going to be retiring, and he knew that he wanted to spend a great deal of his time in retirement giving back to the community. When the time came, he was still thinking about the Oral Lee Brown Foundation. So he talked about it with his wife, Georgia, and then they called the Oakland Unified School District and asked for my phone number. This happened in 2000—the kids were already in college, and at the time I wasn't interested in having more board members. Still, they insisted on meeting with me and talking about what I was doing. So I went to Scott's Seafood in Oakland to meet David Osborne, and to my pleasant surprise I found that he was a wonderful man. We talked for hours about the kids and the foundation, and then he wrote me a large check in support of what we were doing.

"But here's the thing, Mrs. Brown," said Mr. Osborne, as he finished writing the check. "If I give you this, I expect to be involved in your organization."

"Mr. Osborne," I said, "it's completely up to you. If you just want to write a check, the kids and I will be more than happy to take it. And if you want to do more than that, I can find lots of things for you to do. But you think about that carefully, because you're not going to find any glamour if you want to work with us."

But Mr. Osborne didn't care about glamour, and neither did Georgia. Georgia took on all kinds of thankless tasks: mentoring students, developing informational materials, making baskets for the annual banquet. After they'd been around just a couple of months, I couldn't imagine the foundation without them. They weren't afraid to do the dirty work, and their experiences with big business and other charitable foundations meant that they had new ideas to help the kids get through college. As I sat there looking at them, I saw that they were ready to burst with excitement at the thought of doing more. I took that as a good sign.

"So if *I* want to do this again, at my age, I know that you guys must feel that there's more we can do." I had high hopes, but a little doubt as I said this. I could see that the Osbornes were excited, but I knew that the rest of my board members might be feeling a little more hesitant. My first class of babies would start graduating from college the next year. Maybe they had other things that they wanted to do with their time—other children to help or other foundations to support. But I didn't want to work alone—I'd done that for years, and even though I knew I could do it again, it's so much easier to do a program like mine if you've got some support.

I should've known that my board members weren't going to let me down.

"I think I can speak for everyone on this," said Mr. Mitchell, and he glanced around to make sure people were nodding. "If you're ready to start with another class, Mrs. Brown, we're ready too. In fact we've been ready for a little while now."

"Were you guys planning something behind my back?" I asked, and then we all laughed together.

We talked about how we might find and look after a new class of students, and with their help I slowly developed the vision I have to this day.

My plan is that the Oral Lee Brown Foundation will send a new class of students to college every four years. I would love to send a class to college every year, but at the moment I think that a period of four years is the best we can do. The foundation's fairly well known, and that's helped us to raise money. You can tell people all about the great work you're doing until you can't speak anymore, but a lot of the time it doesn't become real to them until they see your organization on TV. For years I had gone door-to-door in Oakland, selling cookies and cobblers and banquet tickets for the foundation, but it was amazing how many phone calls I got from local people after I went on the *Today* show and *Oprah*. "We had no idea this was happening right here in Oakland!" they said. "Can I send you a check?" That made me a little angry, but how could I get upset when they were, after all, offering to help? And I was always pleased to get messages from people all around the country, who had no way of knowing what we were doing here in Oakland. Each time I went on television, we got hundreds of e-mails, dozens of phone calls, and thousands of dollars in donations. The first day after I went on *Oprah*, for instance, we received $20,000 in pledges from across the country.

Despite the attention, we're not yet on the level where we can afford to send kids to college every year. Plus, I like the idea of spending lots of time with the kids and getting to know them well. We want to make sure they get that personal attention so they don't just feel like they're being pushed through the program with no one knowing who they are.

To launch this plan in 2001, the board and I realized that we would need to adopt groups of individual students from three different grade levels: first-graders, fifth-graders, and ninth-graders. If we started with just the first grade, like I had done in 1987, it would be twelve years before we sent a class to college. And if we started with just the upper grades, we wouldn't be preparing younger students to follow the program through high school and on to college.

"It can go on a rotating system," I said. "So every four years, we add another class of twenty first-graders. And then we have a cycle in place, to send kids through high school and on to college."

Of course, that meant that we were going to have to steel ourselves for what one of my board members pointed out during our planning: "Wait a minute, wait a minute. You all realize this means we're *always* going to have sixty students to take care of now?"

When she said that, I felt my head spinning, so I cut in and added, "Yeah, but remember, we're going to set the rules this time." I had some very definite ideas, hard-earned from my experience with the first class, to make our job of looking after sixty kids manageable.

We incorporated these ideas in the application criteria. We wrote that we were looking at income, first of all. I'm not going to pay for a kid whose parents make $100,000 a year. That's not to say that he doesn't deserve to go to college, but I can't be taking care of someone who earns more than I do. So we used the HUD guidelines for what counts as a "low-income" family in Oakland, and said that the child's parents could not be making more than about $25,000 a year.

Besides income, we would be looking for children with good grades. By *good* grades, I don't mean a 4.0. We've got kids in my new class who have a 2.5, and we've got kids who've cracked the 4.0 barrier, by getting all As plus As in honors classes. We've got kids who sail through all their courses and we've got kids who struggle to get a C in math. The point, and I spelled this out in my letters to the teachers and the principals, was that we were looking for students who had a history of making an effort in the classroom. Even if their grades weren't perfect, we wanted them to be self-motivated.

That was really important to me. I'll put it this way: I think my first class went to college because *I* wanted them to go to college. I think my second group will be going to college because *they* want to go to college. I won't have to spend a lot of time convincing them that college is the right thing to do with their lives.

That's not to say that I've given up on kids who don't know if they want to go to college or not. None of us know what the first-graders think of college, nor will we ever know if it's what they want when we take on new classes of first-graders in the future. At the age of six, how can they know what they want to do with their lives? So we'll really have a chance to shape them, but because we were also starting out with ninth-graders, we weren't going to have time to talk them into thinking about college as a positive option for the future. They needed to already believe in it themselves.

The third criteria was parental involvement. I don't think I need to give a lot of explanation for this one: it was my biggest frustration with my first class. It was also the best lesson I learned from that experience: if a kid is going to succeed, his parents can't hold him back. It's unfortunate, but it happens a lot in poor neighborhoods. Some parents get jealous, or they become afraid that their kid is going to become successful and leave them behind. It's the ugliest, most vicious part of the cycle of poverty.

You might be thinking that this criteria is less than fair — after all, some of the best students in my first class came from family situations that weren't just broken up, they were broken *down*. It's a tough one, but the fact of the matter is that I can't do this on my own. What I will say is that we just tried to make sure that the overall class had involved and interested parents — we didn't enforce it to the point where excellent students with unfortunate family problems would be shut out.

We've got one high school student in the program now whose mother greeted us by throwing a shoe out the door when we came to knock. Obviously, we're not going to get a lot of parental support there. But we took the boy anyway, and I'm confident that he's going to be fine.

Finally, we asked the students to write an essay about why they were interested in being part of the program. We knew that the first-graders couldn't do this, so we made a note on the application asking their parents to write an essay about why they were interested in having their child be part of the program. As for the upper grades, we wanted to hear from the kids in their own words what they thought about education and their futures.

Once we had locked in the application criteria, we created a form. And in September 2001, I took that form to Kinko's and made a whole stack of photocopies. With the help of my board members, I passed them out to every principal at every public school in Oakland.

"Tell all your teachers," I told them. "Tell every student you know. We want everyone to know."

"All right, Mrs. Brown," they all said, and for the most part they must have done it: we got over nine hundred applications for sixty positions. The largest number of applicants came for the ninth-grade program. Nearly four hundred fourteen-year-olds in Oakland wrote and asked if the foundation would send them to college.

That may sound like a lot, and I can assure you that it was a lot to process, but I wasn't fazed. To tell you the truth, I was surprised that we didn't get a larger response. I'd lived in Oakland too long to believe that there were only nine hundred students who wanted to go to college but couldn't afford to do so. And sure enough, we started getting angry phone calls soon after we'd made a public announcement of our selections.

"We didn't know," parents and students wailed over the phone.

I patiently explained how we'd sent the information to every school in Oakland, with strict instructions that teachers should identify their low-income students and invite them to apply for the program.

"Well, then, the principal must not have told them to do that," they said, and sure enough I later found out that there were a few principals and teachers who did not do what we had asked them to do. I made a note of those schools and had stern talks with those principals afterward, but there was nothing I could do for the students who didn't get a chance to apply that year.

"I'm really, truly sorry," I told them. "Unfortunately the students have already been selected. But I'll tell you what, I'm going to have a talk with your principal and I suggest you do the same." And some of them did.

I felt awful that some kids didn't get a chance to apply, but unfortunately it wasn't within my powers to make sure that school principals in Oakland cared about the future of their students. Lord knows, I wish it was. But all I could do was concentrate on what *was* within my powers, which was starting the new program.

My board selected the new class. I told them flat-out that I didn't want any part of choosing the applicants. The reason I did that is because I know myself. I'd try to take all nine hundred students, and that's just not feasible. I would have gotten so personally involved with those applications, and so furious at the socioeconomic obstacles keeping the kids from having a bright future, that I would have started trying to figure out a way that we could send them *all* to college. And I knew that that was a losing proposition, so I just took myself out of the process altogether.

First, the board narrowed down the applications to forty in each grade level. I don't know how they did it, so don't ask me. I'm sure they stuck to the guidelines we'd set out to some extent and used their judgment about applicants who looked particularly promising. Then they called in those 120 students—and their parents—for an interview.

As determined as I was to stay out of the process, I couldn't resist the temptation to sit in on the interviews. I wanted to catch a first glimpse of my new class, and I definitely wanted to see their parents. And I'm glad I did. The students were very impressive, and so, for the most part, were their parents. Once again, I was struck by the incredible need within Oakland, and I was even more struck by the fact that this need certainly wasn't confined to East Oakland. We had applicants from all over Oakland, even applicants who went to school in wealthy areas but were not wealthy themselves.

The students came from every sort of family background, every ethnic and racial group. And every single one of them had a hopelessly frustrating economic reason for why they couldn't afford to go to college. Sitting in on those interviews made me feel even more passionate about the decision to take on a second group of students. I knew that I had done the right thing, even if it was going to be exhausting.

After the interviews, the board convened and decided who

were going to be the students in the new program. For the most part, I was happy with their choices. They had a very difficult task—one that would have been impossible for me. So I don't mean to sound ungrateful when I say that there was one choice I wish they had made.

One of the students who was selected for an interview but not selected for the program was a young ninth-grader with a solid, if unexceptional, academic record. She had mostly Cs and Bs and not many extracurricular activities, which I suppose made her a chancy candidate on paper. But when the board read her application, they were struck by the power of her desire to go to college, which was reflected in her essay. And when I met her and her mother in the interview, I started to understand what was going on with her schoolwork.

She was a sweet, smart girl who was slowly being crushed by the weight of caring for four younger siblings. There was no father in the house, and her mother worked all hours of the day and night, so the burden of taking care of these young children had fallen almost completely on this young girl.

Well, no wonder she had mediocre grades and no activities. She didn't have time to do anything after school, including her homework. She was too busy raising her mother's children!

Now, if she had been selected for the program, I would have taken her mother aside for a little talk.

"I need to have a little talk with you about your eldest daughter," I would have said. "I'm having this talk with you because I assume that you want her to succeed."

I would have been very stern with that mother, and I would have let her know that she needed to take some of that responsibility off of that young girl. I am positive that if that mother and I had worked out a solution so that girl would not have to take care of all those children, her grades would have improved. And while I have a lot of sympathy for that mother — I know how hard it is to be a single mother with no support — I also know that raising four younger siblings is a burden that no child should have. If her mother really thought hard about it, she could have found another solution for her child-care problem. And that's what I would've insisted that she do, if we had chosen the girl for the foundation.

As it happens, we did not. I protested about it, because it was the board's opinion that some of those Cs on the girl's report card could have been Bs. As soon as I opened my mouth, they capitulated immediately.

"Well, why don't we bring her on, then?" they said.

"No," I said. "This was your decision and you made it. I'm not going to change your decision, because I can't get involved in this. It's too personal. Besides, I'm sure whoever she would be replacing is perfectly worthy as well. But I just want you to know how I feel about that student, because sometimes you have to look a little deeper at the reasons for why someone doesn't look great on paper."

I didn't say anything more to them about it, but I'm sure that one of the reasons why I fought for that girl is because she reminded me of myself at her age. I don't remember what my grades were like in high school, but I'm sure that they weren't all that they could have been. What if I had found out about a program like the Oral Lee Brown Foundation while I was taking care of all my nieces and nephews? I would have applied in a heartbeat, and no doubt I would have written an essay that was full of passion just as this girl did. Would I have been rejected, too, because I didn't look great on paper?

Eventually, I calmed down about that student. I kept reminding myself that I had given the board the responsibility to select the students, and that it wasn't a task that I would have been able to take on. I have great faith that if this young girl is as resourceful as I believe she is, she's going to be okay in this world. So the board and I put the incident behind us and focused on the new class of students. There are sixty of them altogether—twenty high school students, twenty middle school students, and twenty elementary school students.

I'm using the same meeting format that seemed to work so well with my first class. Every month I hold a group meeting with the students in lower grades and their parents. We use these meetings to talk about what's going on in the classroom and to identify any problems anyone might be having. Every quarter, I get report cards from the young students or their parents, and I sit down with each of them to talk about how things are going in school. All twenty elementary school students come from just two schools, so I've gotten to know their teachers on a first-name basis. I'm not close to any of them the way I was with Mrs. Waters, but I pop in all the time to see how everyone's doing. I can't pop in on the middle school students—they come from seven different middle schools, and they change teachers five or six times a day—but we're on the phone often, and if there's any trouble I'll drive over to that school in a heartbeat.

I'm a little bit stricter with the high school students than I was with my first class. I think that's because, in part, I have less time with these babies, and we have a lot of ground to cover. So we meet in a big group twice a month, and I insist that their parents come along too. We use those meetings to talk about grades and the things that the students need to be doing in order to get ready for college.

There's also—and this is a valuable lesson that I learned from my first class—lots and lots of tutoring for *all* the students. When I created a tutoring program for my first class, they really started to get into their schoolwork. Plus, it really helped them bond.

So now we have tutoring four afternoons during the week for the lower grades and twice a month, on Saturdays, for the high school students. Some of my board members still volunteer with the tutoring program, but increasingly our tutors are retired teachers and other members of the community. That's great, because they've got real expertise with the subjects that the kids are studying in school—and they know the best ways to teach them.

The tutors are just one example of the community involvement we've been able to tap into this time around. It's been truly wonderful to have the community and the kids' parents involved. With the parents, for example, I know when I call a meeting that 90 percent of the parents will be there. With my first class I could only count on maybe 20 percent. Having everyone present means that I only have to say things once. I don't have to spend my time calling every parent at home or trying to track them down at work to let them know that we're going on a field trip— I can use that time planning the field trip instead.

Some of these new parents are so concerned that they'll even pay for a cab to get themselves and their child to a meeting, even though they barely have enough money to pay their own rent. One night I called a meeting for the high school kids with

less notice than usual, but that didn't stop the parents from
making it out anyway—Joanne and I counted three cabs
pulling up to the curb that night. I was shocked. They really
didn't have to do that—they could have called me, or any of the
foundation's board members, and we would have gladly picked
them up. Or they could have sent their kids by themselves, because unlike the younger children, the high-schoolers are old
enough to go out by themselves. In a way it made me feel a bit
bad that they would spend that kind of money on a cab, but on
the other hand, who am I to say that making an investment in
your child's future isn't worth going without a little meat that
week? Because it does make a big difference to the kids—if
they see their parents making those kinds of sacrifices, they feel
an additional incentive to do well.

As for the community, I think they're pitching in for two
reasons: they've heard of the foundation now, and with the
second group, we're taking care of a multiracial group of kids.

Publicity, as much as I hate doing it, has brought some benefits. I'm not just being modest—I really do hate doing publicity. For one thing, I get nervous. I can't remember anything
about what it was like to be on *Oprah* or the *Today* show or
20/20 or all the rest of them, and I refuse to watch the tapes.
The one thing I do remember is that Oprah Winfrey and Katie
Couric really, truly listened to me and my babies while we
were sitting in front of them, and I was very impressed with
both of them. I've been interviewed by a lot of local television
reporters who acted like they were only interested in the camera. I think that's why both of these wonderful ladies got to the
top—they are very sincere. That's not to say that the men who
interviewed me, like Peter Jennings, weren't sincere, because

I believe they were. They were just a little bit more reserved—and I guess as news anchors, they have to be.

In general, though, I don't like answering questions about what I've done—I'd rather be doing it! I've only done one interview that I really enjoyed, and that's because it wasn't an interview at all. It was a conversation. And it was a conversation with one of my all-time favorite celebrities, Bill Cosby. He'd heard about the foundation through the *Today* show and all the media attention we got in 1999, and one of his assistants called and asked if I might be interested in meeting him to talk about what we'd been doing in Oakland.

Well, she certainly didn't need to ask me twice—or even once, for that matter! Before she had finished telling me all the details, I was asking how soon could I meet with him. I have so much respect for Bill Cosby. Even when he first started making a name for himself as a comedian, I appreciated the fact that he refused to use filthy language in his stand-up routines, because he wanted to prove that a black comedian could be funny and successful without it. And of course there was *The Cosby Show*, which was true family entertainment and did so much to improve race relations in this country. I appreciated, too, the fact that he and his wife, Camille, have donated so much time and money to education, especially the historically black colleges.

It was a great conversation. There were cameras there—reporters from local and national media who'd come to write stories about our meeting—but I didn't even notice them. I was completely focused on Mr. Cosby. When he walked in and shook my hand, I didn't know what to expect. Fortunately, in real life he's as down-to-earth and funny as he is on television. He made jokes about casual topics like his show, the weather, and his age, but when it came to the matter at hand he got serious. He asked me the usual questions about how I'd done it and why, but I didn't get impatient because, after all, it was Bill Cosby who was doing the asking. Then he told me how happy he was to see a project like mine, and we talked about what could be done to improve my program and achieve higher educational levels for black people in general. He was of the opinion that we—and he meant we as community members, parents, concerned citizens of all races—have to educate our children as to *why* they need to get an education. We talked a lot about the way the American economy is changing to exclude all but the college-educated.

That conversation had a big impact on my thinking, and I just want to take a moment now to reemphasize this point—*the American economy is changing to exclude all but the college-educated.* It's important to impress that upon our kids, because otherwise they won't understand why it's so important to go through the struggle for an education. Maybe when I was young a man without a college education could still get a union job that paid him enough money to buy a house and raise his kids with some dignity, but those days are over. Most of those jobs—in manufacturing or building or factory work—have disappeared from this country, and they're not coming back. The alternative is dead-end service jobs that just don't pay enough money to raise a family. The other alternatives are crime, or helplessness. And we can't afford to consign our kids to futures like that.

That's the next message I'll be pushing when I do another round of publicity. But for now, we're still getting phone calls all the time from people who say that they heard someone talking about the foundation on the radio or watched a repeat program about us on TV, and could they do anything to help us out? You sure can, I always say, and many of them take my suggestions to help by tutoring or making donations or coming in to speak to the kids.

Aside from the publicity, I think the reason we've gotten a lot of community support this time around is the fact that we've taken kids from all over Oakland. We've got students from every school, every neighborhood, and every ethnic group in Oakland—Mexican, Cambodian, Vietnamese, El Salvadoran. Some of the kids live in strong immigrant communities and those folks are used to pitching in to help one another. Also, and I don't mean to sound racist, but I think people feel a bit more comfortable helping out or donating money when they see you've got a multiracial group as opposed to twenty black faces. I don't get upset about that, though—I maintain that I had to see if I could successfully help my own kids first before I tried to help everyone else's kids.

Parents, community members, sixty kids—that's a lot of people to look after. And I realized pretty quickly that we were going to run into a logistical problem with the tutoring program and all the meetings: Where could we fit everyone? The local public library had been the host of my after-school tutoring sessions for my first class, but as kind as they'd been for all those years, I couldn't ask the library officials to house us anymore. There were just too many of us now. Plus, with the kids coming from all over the city, there was no central library that would be easy for everyone to get to. The problem of centralization also made me rule out the Brookfield Recreation Center—to their relief, I'm sure. To tell you the truth, I hated the idea of being a burden on any community center. I really wanted us to be independent as a foundation, and to always have a place where the kids could come, hang out, and feel safe.

So once again I started looking at what I already had to work with. The answer was literally right next to me.

My real estate office is on 99th Avenue and MacArthur Boulevard. That's the heart of East Oakland—we're surrounded by cheap motels, worn-out shops, and a whole lot of people who hang out on the corners with nothing to do. The environment is part of the reason why I painted the building bright pink. I wanted to bring a little brightness and cheer to the area, which I really do love despite the poverty and hard times.

My office sits right on the corner of 99th, the first of two buildings sitting right next to each other. For years I had worked in the first building while a family lived in the building behind, which had been outfitted to serve as a two-bedroom apartment.

In 1996, that house behind me became available for sale, and I decided it was a great opportunity for me to earn a little extra money. So I bought the house and rented it out to a family who lived there for years. It was a good arrangement because I could keep a careful eye on my tenants, and if there was ever a problem, all they had to do was walk two steps over to my work office and let me know.

But now I started thinking that maybe the house would be just as effective as a home for my foundation. We could hold the tutoring program there after school and on the weekends, with no worries about our group being too big or too loud for a small public space. The board would have a place to meet and discuss things, rather than cramming into one another's houses as we'd done for all these years. We could set up computer terminals in the basement so the kids could learn computer skills on a regular basis. And best of all, the kids would have a place to hang out that had, but was not dominated by, adult supervision.

It would be easier on my real estate business, too, because for years I'd had kids running in there all hours of the day, disrupting my paperwork and disturbing my clients. As much as I love all my babies, I knew that my clients didn't appreciate the ruckus, and I didn't blame them. Buying or selling a house is a serious decision, and when you decide to do it you want a real estate agent who can give you her full attention.

It was a tough decision—it meant displacing my tenants and giving up my investment in the property. I would basically be donating the property to the foundation. But I didn't hesitate for long. In January 2003 I gently informed my tenants that I would be needing the building, and I told them that they needed to find another place to live as soon as possible. It took them about three months to find another home, and it took me and the board members a couple more months to set the house up as a proper working foundation.

We installed computers, most of them donations, in the basement. Helen helped me set up a secretary's desk in what used to be the living room, and I found an old dining room table at a salvage store that we now use as our meeting/tutoring table, next to the kitchen. Upstairs there are two rooms that we use as private tutoring rooms. Just like the foundation, there are no frills, and sometimes we have to improvise. But I think that's a strength—it's made us more creative and efficient.

We opened the new home of the Oral Lee Brown Foundation in April 2003, and it's been one of the best things that's happened for the program in years. It makes a huge difference for us to have a real home, both as a business and as a support network for the babies. My board members and I can hold meetings whenever we want rather than having to work around the schedules of spouses and children who need the living room in our houses. The kids feel comfortable coming in and working on their homework; the tutors feel like they have a place where they can work with no distractions.

I'm retiring this year, and as soon as I do, I plan to turn over my real estate office next door to the foundation too. I've got a vision of joining the two structures together, so that we can have one big room on the top floor for all the kids to sit in together. For space reasons, we can never gather all the kids together for big meetings or fun events, and that's a true shame. The middle-schoolers never get a chance to talk to the high-schoolers, and the elementary school kids don't get to talk to the middle-schoolers. They only see each other twice a year: at the big foundation picnic and the annual fund-raising banquet. I'd love to have a big "Oral B." kids sleepover. I'd love it if the older kids could tutor the younger ones. I'd like it if they could all do computer tutoring at the same time. When I retire and convert the real estate office into the foundation, too, we'll be able to do that.

For now, though, we're doing just fine with what we've got. The kids are just happy to have a building they can go to. The kids we accepted as ninth-graders are getting ready to apply to college now, and I spend a lot of my time with them. They amaze me. To give you an idea of how exceptional they are, I'll just talk a little bit about two of the high school students: Guadelupe Quanteras and Kevin Leslie.

Guadelupe is, plain and simple, an excellent young lady.

She's petite and pretty, with the kind of smile that starts out slow and then takes over her whole face. She smiles a *lot*—it seems to me that she's cheerful and positive all the time. She told me she stays positive for her family, especially her sister. It's just the two of them and their parents, who are poor but proud and determined to see that Guadelupe gets the best future possible. Guadelupe's pretty determined, too. She works as hard on her schoolwork as any student I've ever seen, and she's got the grades to prove it. But she's also a star soccer player on the Oakland Technical High school team. The *Oakland Tribune* did a story on her last year, calling her one of the best high school athletes in the city. She's been approached by quite a few schools who are interested in having her play on their soccer team, but Guadelupe tells them that she's interested in going to a college for its academic programs, not for its soccer team. When I found out that she was telling schools that, I called her myself and told her what a smart young lady I thought she was. A lot of other kids, especially kids with athletic ability, get their heads turned by these Division I schools and completely forget why they should want to go to college in the first place. But not Guadelupe. People tell her to stick her head in the clouds, and she keeps her feet planted right on the ground.

She hasn't let the attention go to her head, either. Guadelupe is also one of the sweetest young women I've ever met. Every week or so she calls me on the phone just to see what she can do to help *me*.

"Mrs. Brown, I was wondering if I could stop by the foundation and give you a hand," she says. "Surely you must have *something* that I can help you with."

"The best way you can help me is to keep right on doing

what you're doing, baby," is what I say in reply. "Don't you worry about me. I'm here to look after you." And I mean it—she needs to worry about her schoolwork, not about what I need to do at the foundation—but I'm always touched when she asks.

Kevin Leslie is a fine young man with the confidence to match—he's slight, and with his height he'll never be the star player on the basketball team, but he carries himself like he's about seven feet tall. And he's generous, just like Guadelupe. Not only does Kevin call me up to ask if there's anything he can do to help out, but his mother and his sister call me too. The way they see it, what's good for Kevin is good for all of them, and I couldn't agree more. It's just the three of them, and they're very close. Mrs. Leslie is a proud, dignified woman. She raised Kevin and his sister all by herself, and she told me once that she used to lie in bed at night and worry herself to pieces over what she was going to do when Kevin was ready to go to college.

"No one's ever helped us before," she said shyly. "And I'm not complaining about that—never have and never will. But I just wanted you to know how much we appreciate what you've done for Kevin. Because I don't know that he would have gotten to college any other way."

"You have no idea how much I appreciate hearing that," I told her. "But I have to tell you that I think Kevin would have gotten to college even if there had never been an Oral Lee Brown. You have raised an incredible young man."

I meant that. Even if we had never sent out those applications, Kevin Leslie would have figured out a way to get through college. He's certainly got the intelligence and the discipline to do so: he's got a 3.5 GPA. He was also selected for the Tuskegee Airmen's special program for Bay Area high school students.

The Tuskegee Airmen were a highly decorated Air Force unit during World War II. All of the pilots were black, and because of segregation they weren't allowed the same opportunities, resources, or training as white pilots. But when it came time to fight, they did much better than those white units. One of the Tuskegee fighter units, for example, didn't lose a single bomber during the whole war. No other fighter unit can claim that level of success.

Some of the original pilots, along with their children and grandchildren, established club associations around the country. Some of the club's branches, including the one in the Bay Area, sponsor programs for promising high school students, teaching them about citizenship as well as giving them the opportunity to learn about aviation. They trained Kevin for hours on a simulator over at Oakland International Airport, and then they told him that he could fly a real plane—if he wanted to. Of course, he jumped at the chance. His instructor told him that there would be a teacher with him in the plane when he flew for the first time, and for days he walked around like he was the happiest kid on earth.

"I'm going to fly that plane, Mrs. Brown," he said.

"You sure are, Kevin," I told him with great pride. It's hard enough for me to think about boarding a plane, much less flying one. So I was happy that he was taking advantage of an opportunity that I will never have. Still, I did have to ask him: "You're not even nervous, Kevin?"

"Oh, I'll do it," he said confidently.

But on the morning that Kevin was scheduled to fly that first plane, he called me.

"I don't know if I'm going to fly that plane, Mrs. Brown," he said gloomily.

"What are you talking about, Kevin?"

"I'm feeling a little nervous."

I had to hold back a chuckle. "Kevin, you don't have anything to be nervous about. You've been practicing for months. Let's not even talk now about how you should have confidence in yourself. Let's talk about your teachers. Do you really think they would let you get in that plane if they weren't sure that you knew what you were doing?"

"No."

"That's right, then. And if they have confidence in you I should think that you'd have some confidence in yourself."

"I do, but—"

"But what, Kevin?"

"It's just the landing that I'm worried about," he said.

"I understand," I told him. "It's just the landing that I'm worried about too, every time I get on a plane. But I'll tell you something, Kevin. Not only are you prepared to do this on your own, but you're going to have someone up in the air with you. One of your teachers. Now, do you think that if, God forbid, anything went wrong, that he would let anything happen to the two of you?"

"I think he'd try to save us," Kevin said.

"That's right," I said. "And I think that, between the two of you, you will find a way to keep that plane in the air and land it safely. And if I know you, Kevin, you're going to do it all on your own, and you're going to do it beautifully."

"Okay, Mrs. Brown," he said.

And he hung up the phone and went over to Oakland International Airport, where, sure enough, he flew that plane without a hitch. He's still flying planes today with the Tuskegee program, and he's gotten even better than ever. I'm not sure if Kevin's planning to be a professional pilot—he's good at so many other things, too—but as I tell him, at least one day he'll be able to fly his own private plane!

So those are just two students from my wonderful new class. All twenty of the high school students are doing well—and so are the twenty elementary students and the twenty middle school students. They're facing the challenges of their environment and their schoolwork with lots of motivation and energy, and for me it's easier this time around. I've already learned some lessons about the best way to run the program. Plus, and it's easy to underestimate this, it's made a big difference for the foundation to have a home. It helps to make us feel that there's some permanence to what we're doing.

Another thing that makes us feel that there's some permanence to the foundation is when one of the members of my first class comes in to check on "the new kids," as they call them. I love to have them come in and talk to the kids or help them out with their homework. I wasn't sure if any of them were going to do so when I first told them that I was taking on a new class, because they were jealous. At least four of my original babies—who shall go unnamed—told me that I shouldn't be taking on a new class.

"You don't need to take on any new kids, Mrs. Brown," they said. "We've worn you out. You need to rest."

"Now, what is this about?" I said. "You know how many kids there are here in Oakland who need my help."

"Yeah, yeah, well," they grumbled.

I pushed them a little bit more and found out that deep down, they were a little nervous that I'd get so busy with the new class that I wouldn't have time for them anymore. Or worse, that I'd come to like the new class better. I told them that their concerns were nonsense, and they came around eventually. They want the new kids to succeed. They even ask me what they can do to help out.

The biggest way they can help out, I tell them, is by serving as role models. My new class has heard all about the first class from the newspapers and from people in the neighborhood, so my first class has taken on the status of legends in the new students' eyes. Robin, LaTosha, and Jeffery have all come in to talk to the new class of high school students, and they've been amazed at how much those kids admire them.

"They think we're heroes or something," Jeffery said.

"Maybe they're right," I said.

"Aww, Mrs. Brown," he said, but he was pleased.

I was pleased, too. As far as I'm concerned, the members of my first class are heroes—my heroes, that is. And they have nothing to fear about losing their place in my heart. As much as I love my new babies, I will never be as close to any children as I am to that first class. We bonded in a way that I don't think will ever happen again, because we had the toughest odds of all. No one thought we could do it. And yes, we proved them wrong. But the best part is that we proved them wrong with nothing but our love and support of one another. That's the greatest success of all.

10

Where They Are Now

The Original Oral Lee Brown Class

To explain why they're my heroes, I'll share a little bit about the progress my first class has made since they graduated from high school.

There's the fact that they graduated from high school at all, of course—every single one of them. As I've said, Castlemont High School had a high dropout rate, but I think it's difficult for people to understand what that means unless they went to a high school like that. What it means is that my babies were watching many of their childhood friends make the choice not to finish school. These were young men and women who they respected and admired, young men and women who they knew were intelligent—and they were telling my babies that high school wasn't necessary. They were telling my babies that they were nerds.

Now, of course my babies had me around to tell them just the opposite, and they believed in themselves, but it was tough to watch everyone around them follow another path. So they had to overcome tremendous stress just to get their high school diplomas. They had to say to their peers, "No, I'm not going to leave. I'm going to go ahead and do this. I do believe in myself, and I believe that by getting this diploma, I'm going to make a better life than what I've had so far." In the ghetto, that's a big leap of faith, and I applaud each and every one of them for having the strength to take it.

After they graduated, nineteen of them went on to colleges in the Bay Area and beyond. Many of them have already finished their undergraduate degrees and everyone who hasn't finished yet is on track to do so soon. At least four out of nineteen are or will be attending graduate school.

I can't even begin to express the pride and joy I felt attending those college graduations. Sure, I was proud and happy at the high school graduations, but I had to be on my best behavior. The world was watching us! So at that first set of graduations, there were no tears and no jumping for joy for Oral Lee Brown.

Fortunately, there wasn't much media attention at the college graduations, so I could whoop and holler as much as I pleased when my babies walked across the stage. I was more relaxed, and some of that had to do with the fact that I could go to all of the college graduations with a lot less stress than the high school graduation. They were in all different parts of the country, sure—but I was used to traveling, especially after I'd helped my babies move all over the country in 1999. The first four college graduations happened over a period of a couple of months, and so I was able to really enjoy some time with my students before their graduations. I also had the opportunity to help them pack up and get ready to leave the place that had been their home for the last four years. And as I did that, believe me, I wasn't the only one who had to choke back some tears.

I'm still waiting to attend quite a few college graduations, and there are a couple of reasons why not all of my babies have finished. We've only had one person who went to college for a couple of years and then decided that it wasn't for him: that's Cory, whom I mentioned earlier. He's since gone on to rescue two people from a fire and is now in training to be a fireman. He said that the discipline he learned in college is helping him now, so even in that case, his education was useful.

Others have either taken time off for personal reasons or haven't been able to get all the credits they needed in order to graduate in four years. That's happened to a lot of my students who are attending California State Universities. California's public universities have suffered lots of budget cuts over the last few years, and as a result they've cut down on course offerings, making it harder for students to get the classes they need to complete their studies. I don't have any power over state budget cuts, and although of course I have some opinions about what the state could cut instead, I keep them to myself. I'm not a political person, although I do think that we should fund our schools a lot better than we're doing right now, especially in the state of California.

As for the ones who have taken time off, usually those personal reasons were family problems, homesickness, or uncertainty that they were doing the right thing by continuing in college. Whenever my babies call me with any of those complaints, I don't argue with them. I voice my opinion: *Are you going to run every time something gets hard? It's not going to get any easier if you leave now.* Then I listen. And if they still tell me that they want to take some time off, we talk about it.

"I'd rather you take a semester off to figure out why you're in college than fail this semester and waste the foundation's money," I tell them. "So let's talk about why you feel this way and what you want to do about it."

Usually they wind up taking off a semester—or even a year, like Michael did—and then going back to school. A few of them, such as Nekita and Michael, have transferred colleges. That makes a tremendous difference, even though they fall behind a little when they change schools. With very few exceptions, the ones who take time off all struggle in the job market for a little while and then wind up wanting to go back to school. When they're ready I help them re-enroll without a word.

They want to go back, they tell me, because college has transformed their lives. They all say that it's been the beginning of their lives. They can imagine futures for themselves that otherwise would have been completely out of the range of their imaginations. They've all got big plans for their lives now, big ambitions, and every single one of them has thanked me for giving them that.

I appreciate their gratitude, but I tell them they should be thanking themselves. I may be responsible for getting them through college financially, but the hard work was done by them, and I tell them so.

"You've created your own future," I say. "I'm here to help you get there, that's all."

But it looks like they're not going to need much help. Jorge Carapia is finishing up his undergraduate work at the University of California at Berkeley in business administration. He's very focused, very determined, and I can see him being the head of a Fortune 500 company one day. Or, if he doesn't want to do that, he'll work for himself. He's got the discipline and the drive to build something from the ground up, and I can see him launching a few successful businesses of his own.

Delisha Cotton is wrapping up her degree at the University of California at Davis. Academically, UC Davis is a great school, but it was not an easy place for a poor kid from Oakland. It's northeast of San Francisco, in a rural area, and when it comes to the students, the per capita incomes are high and the percentages of people of color are low. When I went to visit Delisha there a couple of times, I felt . . . well, uncomfortable isn't the word, but I wouldn't have made it through college there.

In fact, of all of my students, I think the only one who could have made it there was Delisha. She's quiet and cheerful and she's got the ability to fit into environments that have intimidated most of my babies. (Delisha wasn't anxious when we went on field trips, for example, to farms or to big expensive stores outside of East Oakland. A lot of the other kids hung back because they felt shy. Not Delisha.) Not all of her years at UC Davis were easy ones, but she is about to graduate and she is planning to attend graduate school. She wants to go into the medical field but hasn't quite decided on her specialty.

Nekita Noel has finished her undergraduate work at Sacramento State and is attending graduate school at the California State University at Hayward. She's studying criminal justice and social work, and she's interested in starting her own program for underprivileged youth. She's also interested in going to law school, and she may in fact go on to get a law degree after she's finished with her master's degree. Nekita's one of my babies who never even dreamed of hanging out with the wrong crowd. She's so focused that it wouldn't have mattered if she'd been born in East Oakland or Palm Beach: she'd have found a way to pursue her dreams regardless of the obstacles.

Robin Travis is working toward her associate degree at American River College in Sacramento. Robin has struggled a lot over the years, and I'm extraordinarily proud of her. She doesn't like being a student—she never has—but she's hanging in there, and just like she graduated from high school in spite of tough odds, she's going to graduate from college. She's worked as a nurse's aide and really enjoyed it, and I believe her goal is to be a nurse herself. I don't think she's going to go on to graduate school right away. Knowing Robin, she'll probably get out into the workforce for a few years, realize that she could be making more money and be happier as an RN, and go back to school. And when she does that she'll get through her studies methodically and with determination, just like she's doing now. Her baby girl is in elementary school and doing just fine.

Robert Porter has just finished his degree at Southern Baton Rouge University. Like Jorge, he's business-minded, but I can't see him running his own company. I don't mean that as an insult—Robert's got lots of abilities and he will probably want to work at the type of big, thriving organization that will give him an opportunity to use all of them. Plus, Robert's a people person, and running your own business is lonely. He's always got a smile and lots of conversation for everyone, whether it's for the CEO of a company or a homeless man on the street.

Winter Woods went to Chabot College and then transferred to a community college close to home. She's had a tough time in college, but she's sticking it out. She's right up there with Robin when it comes to determination.

Taisha Lomack is also going to a community college close to home — Contra Costa College, which is a couple hours' drive north of Oakland. Tish Beverly went to Laney College in Oakland, and she's currently working for the City of Oakland. She and Taisha both hope to get their bachelor degrees, even if it takes them a while.

Kela Harris and Krystal Cunningham are both almost finished with their undergraduate work at Howard University in Washington, D.C. Usually I hear from them twice a year through the mail: certified packets containing their grades for that semester. I always suspect when I pick up those packets that the grades are going to be excellent, and I'm always right.

I see Curtis Richardson fairly frequently, because he's attending cooking school in the area. Sometimes he'll have me over when he's "practicing" for a test. The first time I went over to his test kitchen, he was testing appetizers, such as bruschetta and mini-soufflés. As I rolled out of that kitchen, I told Curtis that I'd be willing to help him test things anytime. He laughed at that. "Okay, Mrs. Brown," he said. "I'll call you next time." He's stayed true to his word, and whenever I get a call I find a way to squeeze it into my schedule.

LaQuita White has just graduated from San Jose State with a major in business and a minor in real estate. Of all my babies, Quita is the only one who's shown an interest in real estate. She didn't show any interest in it during high school, but around her sophomore year in college she took a class and really enjoyed it. During her senior year she asked me to train her as an agent and a broker, and I was surprised and pleased. I haven't trained new employees in decades, and I'm about to retire, but I told Quita that I'd make an exception for her. We're going to start working soon, and I think she's going to be a great trainee. Quita doesn't ever want to be second at anything, which is the mind-set a great real estate agent needs to have. So I'm looking forward to working with her. I think the experience will be a great way to conclude my own real estate career.

Michael Tatmon and LeAndre Miller are still pursuing professional careers in basketball. Michael's almost finished his degree at Cal State Hayward, and LeAndre is wrapping up his last year at Delta College in Stockton. Both of these fine young men have frustrated me to no end over their college years, but that's only because I love them both so much. "I know you love basketball more than anything," I've told them, over and over again. "But what are the odds? Do you know how many kids want to be in the NBA?"

"Yeah, I know, I know," they both say.

They both love basketball more than anything. They always have. Even when we went on field trips in elementary or middle school, they always brought a basketball along. We'd be walking down the street on the way home from school, and they'd be bouncing a basketball or practicing their footwork. So I know they love it, but I also know the odds. I'm just thankful that they both have college degrees, and they're both bright young men with plenty of options if they don't make it to the NBA.

LaTosha is doing graduate work in accounting at Jackson State University in Mississippi. She's a rising star—last summer she had an internship with the top accounting firm right here in Oakland. Jeffery's another one. He's determined to be a major entrepreneur in the music business. Even before he graduated from Columbia College in Chicago, he'd set his heart on getting into the MBA program at the University of California at Los Angeles. After graduation, he packed his things and moved to Los Angeles, only to find out that UCLA doesn't accept new graduates into its MBA program. That news might have deflated most people, but not Jeffery. He decided he'd come too far to let that stop him, so he's working and taking classes at UCLA's extension school in order to get experience to reapply for his MBA in a year or so.

The last of my babies who is still in college is Erica Lincoln. For two reasons, she is working at Federal Express while she goes to community college: she's looking after her family, which needs her financial support, and, like Robin, school is not the most enjoyable thing in the world for her.

"It's hard, Mrs. Brown," she's told me.

"I know, baby," I said. "But it'll be easier if you just knuckle down and finish."

"I'm going to finish," Erica said. "I haven't dropped out yet, and you can believe that I don't intend to ship boxes for the rest of my life."

I do believe her. Erica's never said anything that she didn't mean, and I know that she knows the value of an education. All she has to do is look at some of her foundation brothers and sisters, like LaTosha or Jorge or Jeffery. None of them will be shipping boxes, because they've got their degrees.

But even my students who didn't go to college have told me that they're doing a lot better than they would have been doing if I hadn't come into their lives. Everyone is working, even if they don't have the jobs they might have had if they had gone to college. They still have better jobs and more self-esteem than they would have had if they hadn't graduated from high school.

Even so, the jobs that are available for high school graduates in the Bay Area now don't come close to the ones that were available when I was a high school graduate here in the 1960s. Now you need a college degree or special high-tech skills just to get in the door. And even that's not a guarantee: when the Internet bubble burst in 2000, it took a lot of Bay Area jobs with it. Most of them haven't come back: there are still a lot of computer engineers and programmers out of work, so you know it's got to be hard for a high school graduate. I think that my students are starting to realize that without higher education, things aren't going to get easier for them—in fact, they're going to get worse. At least two of my students who decided not to go on to college directly after high school—Susan Richards and LaQuanda White—have called me and told me that they're thinking of applying after all.

"Go ahead and do it," I said. "As long as I'm alive and breathing, the foundation will be here, and we'll pay for you to go."

So far, they haven't applied, but the seeds have been planted in their mind, and I think that's all right. The fact that they're thinking of going to college, that they can see a way to a better job and a higher salary through education instead of swallowing some mediocre job for the rest of their lives, shows me that I've been successful.

But—to me—the biggest sign of my success is the fact that nearly every one of my babies who left Oakland for college plans not to return.

That sounds bad, so let me add that I don't mean they plan to forget where they came from! I've told all of them many and many a time that I didn't raise any spoiled kids who think they can leave the ghetto and forget all about the people who are still struggling here. I've said to them, "If you turn your back on the people of East Oakland then you're turning your back on me. And don't think I won't go and find you up in your big house in the hills!"

"Aww, Mrs. Brown," they say, and then we all laugh.

Because I know, and they know, that just because my babies are leaving Oakland doesn't mean that they're never going to give back to the people here. Jeffery has already told me that he can't wait until he has enough money to contribute to the Oral Lee Brown Foundation, and some of my other students who have graduated, like Nekita and LaTosha, come in and help out all the time. But they don't plan to live in East Oakland anymore, and I believe that means I've met my goal.

I try to convince people in the community that they should be supportive of anyone who manages to get out. Look up to them as role models, I've said. But not enough people share my attitude, and in some cases it's made life rough on my babies when they *have* tried to come back and share their experiences with the community.

To give you an example, let's take my baby Nekita. Now,

Nekita's one of the sweetest young women you can imagine. She's not the type to give anyone any drama or any—well, I won't say any, but I'll say any *unnecessary*—attitude. She came home to Oakland for the summer after her sophomore year in college, and one day she called me nearly in tears.

"Calm down, baby, calm down," I said.

"Everything's wrong," she sobbed. "All these girls over here are saying I think I'm better than they are because I went to *college* and now they're telling these other girls over here—"

"Slow down," I said. "Why don't you start at the beginning?"

Nekita had gone out with some of her old friends from high school. These girls had not been fortunate enough to have the chance to go to college. Their lives had, to put it politely, stalled. Many of them were working, but the jobs they had—working at McDonald's or Kinko's or selling clothes at Bayfair Mall—didn't have much in common with Nekita's plans to be a criminal psychologist. Some had already had babies, and some weren't working at all.

Now, I know Nekita didn't view them any differently because their lives had gone in another direction than hers. But Nekita did view certain activities differently than she used to. These girls wanted to go to a club that they had all been going to since Nekita went off to college, and Nekita didn't like the sound of the place. She'd heard that there had been some fights there recently, and she didn't want to be involved in any of that. If something happened, she didn't want to be caught in the crossfire. So she told the girls that she wasn't interested in going.

That's when they started talking about her.

"Oh, you think you're something now that you're in college," they said. "You think you're any better than the rest of us just because you run around with all those rich kids now? You think you're different?" They said mean stuff like that. It hurt Nekita's feelings so bad that she left and ran right over to her sister's house, and that's when she called me.

"You know what, Nekita," I said, as she was blowing her nose. "I'm going to tell you something straight about what just happened, and don't you let it go to your head. You listening?"

"Yes," she sniffled.

"Good. Now, first of all, they're right," I said. "You are different. They don't understand you anymore. They're still sitting here in East Oakland, working mediocre jobs, having babies, doing whatever it is they're doing, and you're not. You have left that world behind. Are you following me?"

"Yes."

"Now, you're nice enough not to say it like I just did, but the fact of the matter is that you see the world a little bit differently than they do right now, and it comes out in your behavior," I said. "They don't like that."

"But I'm not saying anything bad about them," she said.

"I know you're not," I said. "You don't have to. They feel bad that they haven't gotten on with their lives like you have, but rather than doing something about it, they're going to sit back and say bad things about you. Now, is that fair?"

"No."

"It's sure not," I said. "It's ignorant is what it is. And you don't need to buy into that. When they say, oh, you think you're this, you just remember—no, you don't *think* you're this, you *are* this. You're a college student. And you don't need to feel any shame about carrying yourself accordingly. Is that clear?"

"Yes."

"You sure?"

"Yes, Mrs. Brown, it's clear," she said.

"All right," I said. "I don't mean that you need to act like you're better than your friends, either. Always respect people. Don't look down on them. They didn't have the same opportunities that you did, but that doesn't mean that you're better than they are. It's just that you have different thinking patterns now. You're focused on the big picture, and they're still looking at street-level stuff. That's what you've been trying to get *away* from."

"Yeah, but I don't want that to mean that I can't be friends with them anymore," she said.

"Well, Nekita, it's hard, but the reality is that you may not be able to," I said. "It's not just because you went to college and they didn't, it's because your interests have changed. And you'll go through this over and over again with your friends throughout your life. It's hard, but that's reality."

So that's what I told her, and in fact one of those summers when the kids were home from college, I had to tell the same thing to Jeffery. Jeffery was trying to spend the summer between his sophomore and junior years working a regular job in Oakland, but he ran into some of his old friends from high school—and they wouldn't accept the fact that he didn't hustle anymore. Jeffery's case was a little bit more serious than Nekita's—the tension between him and his old friends got so bad that I had to buy him a plane ticket and send him back to Chicago. His old friends were leaning on him to get involved in some of their old activities, and he really didn't want to get caught up in that again.

"Can you help me, Mrs. Brown?" he said.

"Jeff, you have to stop hanging out with these people," I told him, and after I gave him the same talk I'd given to Nekita, I bought him a plane ticket and sent him back to Chicago.

My babies were all right, but I'm telling you these stories because what happened to them happens to bright, poor kids all over the country. Usually they get held back before they even have a chance to get to college. Most of the time they don't get the chances they should get in life because the opportunities just aren't there, and they don't have any support from mentors or role models. But sometimes they get held back because people in their own communities—friends and family—don't want them to succeed. They put them down and discourage them out of their own insecurity, telling them that they're nerds, or that they think they're better than someone else, even threatening them. It's vicious, and the saddest thing about it is that some of these communities are just perpetuating a culture of failure.

Fortunately, my babies had a lot of inner strength to draw on, and they had me breathing down their necks if I heard any self-doubt. They know their opportunities, and they know their responsibilities. They are going to be just fine, and I am so proud of them.

∝

As for me, I'm doing quite well myself. It's time for me to retire from real estate and get on with the next phase of life. All my friends tell me that retirement isn't nearly as boring as they were brought up to believe it was, and I'm looking forward to finding out if they're right. Somehow I doubt that my new life as a retiree will be much slower than my life as a member of the workforce has been!

Besides taking a vacation every once in a while, I've got lots of plans for what I can do for the foundation after I retire. Some of those plans are small, like figuring out how the foundation can replace the $10,000 that I've been donating from my salary every year. The $10,000 that I used to donate in the 1980s doesn't go nearly as far toward a college education now, but it's still $10,000 that we can't afford to lose. Fortunately, the foundation has gained lots of donors besides me, but I don't want to retire without replacing that source of income.

My solution is to donate something else instead: my time. Ever since my first class graduated from high school in 1999, I've gotten speaking requests from people and organizations all over the country. All sorts of community-service groups and membership organizations want Oral Lee Brown to speak at their national banquet about how to help poor kids become interested in education. When I first got these phone calls, I was just bewildered.

"What do you mean, you want me to come speak?" I said. "I'm just Oral Brown, another name, face, and social security number. I can't tell you all the answers."

As hard as it is to believe, I'm actually a very shy person. And even though I've given interviews on national television and I always give a speech at the foundation's annual banquet—a good one, I'm told—there's still a part of me that's shy about getting up in front of crowds like that. I guess that deep down, I still think of myself as just that poor little girl from Mississippi who always got hushed whenever she tried to speak up.

So I never went to the big banquets and functions; I never gave any of the speeches that I was asked to give. Part of it was that I'm shy, but the other part of it was that I never had the time. But once I'm retired, I'll have the time and the flexibility to give some of these speeches, and I think that's how I'll make up my annual $10,000 donation. Quite a few of the organizations I've spoken to have said that they'd be willing to pay me $10,000 for a single speech. As long as they're willing to write that $10,000 check to the foundation instead of me, I'm willing to go to their banquet and give a speech. Because I don't need the money and have never needed the money. I'd much rather give it to my babies.

I'll give speeches, and I'll put more time into planning our annual banquet. We still hold our fund-raising banquet every fall in Oakland, and every year we've raised more and more money for the kids. Over time, especially as the board of the foundation became more active, we've introduced silent auctions and special sales at the banquet to raise additional money. They've been very successful, but my hunch is that I'll be able to throw an even better party once I retire.

Planning a banquet takes a lot of time, energy, and creativity. Even though we've been holding good ones since 1988, I think that once I can dedicate a lot of time to them, they're going to be *huge*. I'm not going to tell you about all of the things I have in mind for the banquets—I can't give away *all* my secrets—but I do suggest that you start calling the foundation months ahead of time if you want tickets.

We're going to need the extra money. Not only is the foundation struggling to keep up with sixty students now instead of twenty-three, but we're making structural adjustments to the way the program is run. I'm serious about converting my real estate office into part of the foundation, and that's going to be very expensive.

Plus, as the foundation gets better known, people are offering my babies more and more opportunities. Sometimes those opportunities are cost-free, but sometimes they're not, and I'd like to give my students as many of them as possible without worrying about the cost. A couple of years ago, for example, I got a call from a program coordinator at the University of California at Santa Barbara. She had heard about the foundation and wanted to offer my new class of high school students the chance to attend a special program that she'd designed just for us.

During spring break, while the college students at UC Santa Barbara were gone, my students would have the campus all to themselves. They'd stay in the dorms, use one of the libraries, and—most importantly—take college classes. The program coordinator had already spoken to several professors, and all of them were eager to teach my students during their week off.

It sounded wonderful, but it wasn't free. It wasn't even cheap—the professors were willing to donate their time, and the program coordinator had asked for donations wherever she could, but between the cost of keeping part of the university open and the cost of transporting all of my students to Santa Barbara and back, I was looking at a bill of $12,000. There was no way that we could afford it.

But I didn't give up. I made applications to various grant foundations and eventually got a $10,000 grant from Shell Oil's charity fund. The foundation kicked in the last $2,000, and twenty of my babies spent an incredible week at UC Santa Barbara. I was thrilled that they got the opportunity to go after all, but I'd like the foundation to have enough money so that we're not scrambling when we're offered opportunities like that.

That's in the short term. My long-term plans are much, much bigger.

People always ask me what I'd like to see for the foundation in the next ten years, twenty years, thirty years. My short answer to that is this: "I'd like to see the foundation disappear."

What I mean by that is that I'd like it if the work that we're doing at the Oral Lee Brown Foundation becomes unnecessary. I'd like it if the work that we're doing would be picked up by not just neighborhood groups and community associations but society itself. If a college degree is necessary to succeed in the American economy, then why is it that college degrees are so difficult to get? Why is it that the only people who can afford a college degree are the wealthy?

I'd like to see a society that's willing not just to say that our current educational system is failing but that will take steps to fix it. If a college degree is necessary, then it should be *necessary* for kids to get one. Ideally, I'd like it if the four years it takes to get a college degree were simply added on to the four years it takes to get a high school diploma. I'd like it if the undergraduate years were part of the public school system the same way that high school is—and if we enforced a rule that said a kid couldn't enter the workforce until after he'd graduated from the sixteenth grade. If that happened, then there would be no need for the Oral Lee Brown Foundation. I wouldn't have to worry about flying all over the country to be congratulated for doing something to help poor kids, because we'd all be doing it.

But what are the chances of that happening? I know they're slim, so I concentrate on the other long-term plans I have for the foundation.

As long as the foundation has to exist, I'd like to help other communities launch their own educational programs. One of the best ways to do this is by using the structures that are already in place—particularly the large ones that already have lots of members. If we could convince big companies or national membership organizations to make education fundraising a priority, then poor communities all over this country would benefit.

Let's say the corporate headquarters of Wal-Mart, or Microsoft, or General Motors asked every one of their employees to donate a single dollar from their paychecks once a year. Just one dollar. People always say that they can't afford to donate to charity, or that they can't pay $50 for a ticket to one of my banquets, but I think that if they're working, they can afford to give $1 once a year. It's not a lot of money to each employee—but it would mean hundreds of thousands of dollars, and possibly millions, for education. If each and every one of those companies did that every year, in ten years there would be enough to send not just my students to college but all the poor kids in East Oakland to college, and probably all of the poor kids in their communities too.

It doesn't just have to be big companies, either. And it

doesn't necessarily have to be about education. I'd love to see the National Rotary Club ask each member to pay an additional dollar for their annual dues every year and then give that money to Alzheimer's patients. I think it would be a wonderful thing if the California Teachers' Union charged an extra dollar a year and gave all the money to diabetes research, or AIDS orphans. The point is, if we all give a *little* it will add up to a *whole lot,* and *it's not that hard.* If I could send all these kids to college on my own, imagine what this whole country could do if we decided to work together.

I'm busy developing a curriculum for people who want to repeat what I did with the Oral Lee Brown Foundation. I've gotten lots of calls from people who are interested in setting up educational foundations and making promises to some of the poor youth in their neighborhoods, and I'd like to share my experiences with them.

I like to help people informally, too. Over the last few years I've given advice to a lot of people who want to make their own promises. I'm happy to report that quite a few of them have launched their own community programs. I'm still in touch with a few of them, like Gordon Faulk, in Milwaukee, Wisconsin, and Hope Hernandez, who's right up the road from me in Vacaville, California.

Gordon has launched an Oral Lee Brown–style program for a second-grade class in Milwaukee, and Hope is in the process of starting her own for Latino children in Vacaville. There's also a group in Oklahoma that has started a mentoring program with fifth-graders. We talk on the phone every so often just to check in and share tips about our babies. I've been through the fight that they're going through right now, and I didn't have much help or understanding from the people around me, so I'm glad that I can be there to offer support for them.

There are others, too. I continue to get phone calls from people in various parts of the country who want to start programs in their communities. Whenever they call me, I ask them first if they've got at least half an hour to talk. If they don't have it right then, or if I don't, we schedule a time when we both do. I call them back, and I start talking.

"I'm thrilled to hear from you," I say. "I mean, I am really excited. Because I'm going to tell you a lot about how a program like this works, and not all of what I'm going to tell you is going to be something that you want to hear."

I tell them everything that happens after the television crews go home. I tell them about the midnight phone calls from kids who are threatening to run away from home. I tell them about the inevitable disruptions to their businesses, their families, their relationships. I tell them about buying students food and clothes and shoes, instead of buying something for themselves. I tell them how people will taunt them or abandon them because they're focused on getting their students through college. I tell them about ungrateful parents and indifferent teachers, and I tell them about students who get angry for no reason at all. I tell them about hurt and disappointment. I tell them about fear and self-doubt.

When I'm all done telling them that, there's always silence on the other end of the phone. So I fill that silence by telling them one more thing.

"There are no television crews around to film the tough parts," I say. "Peter Jennings isn't going to pop up when you've just worked a twelve-hour day and have to go rescue one of your students from their house because they just got in a fight with one of their parents. In fact, he may never pop up at all. So don't do this expecting any recognition."

"Well, Mrs. Brown," I remember one woman saying to me at this point in the conversation. "This *is* discouraging. Are you trying to talk me out of starting this program, or what?"

"I'm not trying to discourage you at all," I told her. "I'm trying to tell you the truth, because I don't want you going into this wearing rose-colored glasses. And what I'm trying to tell you is that it's hard, harder than you can possibly imagine right now. But the other part of the truth, and it's something that I can tell you in the same breath, is that sending kids to college is more wonderful than you can ever imagine."

I meant that, too. Even though adopting these kids and sending them off to college has been the hardest thing I've ever done, it's also been the best thing I've ever done. As I like to tell people, it was my mission from God, but it was also my pleasure. I've experienced tears and pain, but also laughter and joy. And I've learned the best way to help kids who have nothing find their way to success: give them the only thing that we all need, which is love.

Oral Lee Brown's Tip Sheet
for College Acceptance

Since every child can't be an Oral Lee Brown kid, here are some pointers and tips that will help students and parents maximize the chance of getting accepted to college.

1. Preparation starts in the first grade.

First of all, go to school. That sounds self-explanatory, but a child starts getting prepared for college the moment he or she sets foot in a classroom. So if you're a parent, don't let your child talk you into letting him stay home unless he's got an excellent reason, like illness. Don't keep him home because you're busy that day and can't get him to school, or because you need him to look after his little siblings because the babysitter didn't show up. Those are *your* problems. Don't let them interfere with your child's responsibility, which is to go to school. Emphasize that to your child—tell him that you have to work, and *his* job is to go to school.

If you're a child, learn all that you can while you're in school. Consider it your job and don't skip school unless you're ill. Ask yourself every morning when you wake up,

"What can I learn today?" When you get to college, some of your classmates may have gone to expensive private schools where they had a lot more resources than you did, so push yourself to do the most challenging work available.

Resources for Tip 1

- The National Parent-Teacher Association regularly publishes information about how to help your young child succeed in school. Contact them at 330 North Wabash Avenue, Suite 2100, Chicago, Illinois 60611, or 1–800–307–4PTA. Their website has lots of helpful information: www.pta.org.

- For young students with computer access, rather than playing video games, look at www.FunBrain.com. There are lots of games here, too, and they'll help you learn.

2. Take control of your own or your child's education.

Once again, this is something that starts in the first grade. If you or your child is attending a public elementary school, my guess is that there's a fight for resources going on somewhere within the administration. Make sure that you're on the winning end of that fight by demanding the best for your child or yourself.

Getting involved in the life of the school is a good way to find out what kinds of programs are on offer and who the best teachers are. Parents should go to teacher-parent meetings. Volunteer in your child's classroom. If you like your child's teacher, ask her who should teach your child for the next few grades. Teachers know their colleagues' abilities like no one else. They also know the school district, and they might be able to steer you in the direction of a good middle school or high school.

If you don't like your child's teacher, sneak over to other classrooms. Spend some time observing the other teachers who are teaching the same grade—you'll quickly see who is a better teacher than the others.

Once you know who's going to be best for your child, make your presence known in the principal's office. Be kind, but firm, when you're insisting that your child has the opportunity to be taught by the best teachers that the school has to offer. You may run into some static from the principal's office, but in my experience a principal will eventually see what she can do to please an insistent parent. Remember that the squeaky wheel gets the grease.

Also, find out if your child's school has an accelerated program for gifted students. If they do, demand that your child be tested for it. Unfortunately, there are a lot of teachers who don't think to recommend poor students and students of color for these accelerated programs. You and your child have to take control of your child's education.

Resource for Tip 2

- The Family Education Network has designed their programs, especially their website—http://fen.com— to help parents and students take control of their education. You can also contact the company directly at 20 Park Plaza, 12th Floor, Boston, Massachusetts 02116.

3. Students: Stay true to your goal.

If you grow up in a poor neighborhood and want to go to college, the obstacles you will face will be harder to overcome than they are for someone who grows up in a middle-class neighborhood. Accept that from the outset and don't dwell on it. You're going to need all your energy to achieve your goal. Remember that you may be disadvantaged economically, but you're not disadvantaged in any other way.

I'll give you an example: most college applications demand that students list their extracurricular activities. If you're poor, you'll be competing with students whose parents have paid for them to take ballet lessons and piano lessons since they were in kindergarten. You won't have that, and chances are that your school won't offer much in the way of extracurricular activities, either.

Rather than throwing up your hands, though, you need to be creative. If you're interested in ballet lessons, for instance, ask yourself, "How can I take these lessons anyway?" Start asking at your church and in your community center. You might find a local Boys and Girls Club that offers ballet lessons, or learn about a community program to teach economically disadvantaged children about dance.

You'll have to do the homework yourself, rather than depending on your parents, family members, or friends to do it for you. But that will give you an edge on other candidates, because you'll learn self-reliance, persistence, and dedication.

Don't give up because you run into resistance in your own community, either. You'll probably hear throughout your childhood that you're a nerd for wanting to go to college.

Other kids will tease you for studying, and maybe even your own parents won't understand your goals. But remember what I always tell my babies: Everyone is an individual. You don't have to stay in the ghetto just because your friends will. You don't have to be content with mediocre jobs for the rest of your life just because your parents were.

Don't listen to any negativity and don't let anyone distract you from your goal. I'm not saying it will be easy, but there is a long, hard road to success, and it's called sacrifice. Be prepared to take it.

Resources for Tip 3

- *Lean on Me* (1989) is a great movie based on a true story and starring Morgan Freeman as a high school principal who helps poor students believe in their school and themselves. I've shown it to all my students starting in middle school. It's an inspiration to me to this day.
- Another great film that helps to motivate young students is *Stand and Deliver* (1988). Edward James Olmos stars as a Los Angeles high school teacher who helps his class beat the odds and learn calculus. This film is also based on a true story, so you can tell your kids that if the kids in these movies could do it in real life, they can do it too.

4. Get involved in your community as early as junior high school.

Colleges require that high school students be involved in community service these days, but that's not the only reason why I'm advocating it. Community service is a great way to get to know the people around you and learn some new skills in the process. Plus, it's free—and you'll likely get back more than you give.

Even when you're in junior high school and can't get around by yourself, there are lots of things you can do. Ask if you can volunteer in your school by working in the library or the cafeteria. If you're in seventh or eighth grade, you may be able to help tutor the younger students. Or you can offer to help your teachers grade papers or set up the classroom. While you're there, talk to them about what you can do to improve your grades. That's a clear situation where everyone wins.

When you get into high school, look for service options that are structured. Your school may offer a community service club or program. If they don't, you can start by asking the local branch of a big, national volunteer organization like the Red Cross. If you attend a church, your church leaders will know about service opportunities. And if you're still stuck, I've never seen a city, town, or village in this country that didn't have a soup kitchen or a senior citizens' home. They are just a couple of the places that *always* need help.

Resources for Tip 4

- To find your nearest Boys and Girls Club of America, call 1–800–854–CLUB.

- You can find a local branch of the Red Cross through their website, www.redcross.org. A local branch will probably also be listed in your phone book.

5. As soon as you get to high school, focus on your grades.

That's when they really start to count. The college admissions officers look at your grades dating from the first day you enter the ninth grade.

Don't fall into the trap of just paying attention to the subjects that you enjoy. College entrance judges look at your performance in English, math, science, history, and foreign languages. I've never met a student who enjoyed all of these subjects equally, but you have to show competence in all of them to get into college.

Get tutoring in the subjects that you struggle with. I was able to set up a tutoring program for my students, but with a little research, you can find free tutoring. Check at your local library, ask your teachers, and ask at the community center. If you've got a Boys and Girls Club in your town, or a YMCA, these organizations often have tutoring, too.

You should also ask your teacher for extra help. Many teachers are surprised and pleased when a student expresses interest in understanding what they're being taught. Quite a few of them will be willing to work with you one on one. Those who can't may be able to recommend a tutor.

By this age you should be able to take some responsibility for your own education. Make sure that you're getting what you need from your teachers. I'm sorry to say it, but not all teachers can teach. If you're unlucky enough to have one of those—or worse, if your teacher doesn't like you and you haven't done anything to provoke her—request a transfer to another classroom. You can't afford to waste your future because of someone else's incompetence.

Resources for Tip 5

- The best advice is to do your work, no matter how hard it is. The best resource you can use during this period of your life is the support of a good mentor. If you can't find one at your school, seek role models at your church or community service activity.

6. Study for the Scholastic Aptitude Test (SAT) like you'd study for a final exam.

Think of the SAT as your college entrance exam, because that's what it is. I like to see students start to study for it as early as the eighth grade.

Get an SAT practice book. You can buy one at the bookstore or find one at the library. The SAT changes every year, but the test focuses on a variety of exercises in math and English. There are certain types of exercises that are on every test every year, so work through the practice exercises and find out where you're struggling. Once you've figured out where your weaknesses are, focus your attention on them — but remember that what matters is your overall score, so *don't forget to study for the rest of the test, too.*

You can take the SAT more than once. I strongly encourage my students to do so. Colleges only ask for your best score, so take the test as many times as you can.

Some students may do better on the ACT, which evaluates creative skills as well as performance in math and English. That's not to say that the ACT is easier. You still need to study for it. Also, not all colleges accept ACT scores, so check with your college of choice to see if they will accept it instead of the SAT.

Resources for Tip 6

- *10 Real SATs*. The College Board. 3rd Edition. New York: College Board Press, 2003. www.collegeboard.com
- *Kaplan SAT Verbal Workbook*. Kaplan. 4th Edition. New York: Kaplan Press, 2002. www.Kaplan.com
- *Kaplan SAT Math Workbook*. Kaplan. 4th Edition. New York: Kaplan Press, 2002.
- Also, keep neighborhood organizations and churches in mind. These places often sponsor SAT study groups. Check bulletin boards and ask officials at your local library, community recreation center, and church.

7. Start thinking about what you want out of a college early in high school. Get informed on what colleges have to offer by going to local campuses and seminars.

I took my first group of students on a college tour, but I know that's not an option for everyone. Fortunately, lots of colleges will come to you as part of a touring seminar—if you keep your eyes open for them.

I like to see kids attending college seminars as early as the ninth grade. Every year, college recruiters and admissions officers tour the country to talk with aspiring college students. They're usually held on the weekends. If it's a big seminar, it will likely be in a hotel, and smaller ones are often held in local churches or community centers. Here in Oakland I've got my high school students signed up for three different seminars: one that's being given by UC Berkeley, one for historically black colleges and universities, and one for the California State Universities. There are others, too, and I encourage the kids to find out and go on their own.

You can find out who's coming to town in a variety of ways. If you've got your eye on a particular college or university, call the admissions office or have a look at their website. There should be information about the places the college is planning to send representatives to meet prospective students, and you might get lucky. Otherwise, keep your eyes on your local newspaper—there's often an ad. Ask at your local university, college, or community college. And make sure you tell your teachers that you're interested in hearing about these opportunities. Often the seminar organizers tell local high schools when they're coming.

Try to find out something about the colleges before you go to the seminar. Use the Internet at your local library and look at their web page. Look at the majors they offer, and notice what the school focuses on. Look for schools that match up with the sorts of subjects and activities that you want to pursue.

When you go to the seminar, take your last report card with you. The recruiter can usually tell you whether or not you have a chance of getting into his school just by looking at your report card. Spend some time talking to each recruiter from the school that you're interested in—they'll be able to give you specialized advice about your application. You might also want to ask about extracurricular activities, the college's student body, and the local community. All of those things are very important when it comes to picking a college where you'll be happy.

Resources for Tip 7

- *Black Excel African American Student's College Guide: Your One-Stop Resource for Choosing the Right College, Getting In, and Paying the Bill.* Isaac Black. New York: John Wiley & Sons, 2000. This book is a few years old, so double-check all the addresses, contact names, and phone numbers before you send away for information and waste your postage. This book is still an excellent resource for helping you figure out what sorts of things to look for in a college. There are multicultural student college guides, too.

- Look for freebies. I found a guide to historically black colleges and universities published by *Ebony* magazine and Chevrolet. It was thin, but it was full of great information about the colleges. Your college counselor should have some of these.

- Call the colleges that you're interested in and request a brochure about the school. Some of them will even be willing to send you a course catalog: just ask.

8. *The process of applying to college is like having a part-time job. Be prepared to give it that much attention.*

The first time I ran the program, my students were amazed at how strenuous the college application process was. So was I. This time I'm better prepared, and I can guide my students through it with relative ease. But I'll tell you the same thing I'm telling them: during the first part of your senior year, you're going to have a part-time job in addition to your schoolwork, your extracurricular activities, and, if you work, your first part-time job. It's the sacrifice you have to make in order to reach your goal.

What goes into that part-time job? For starters, keeping your grades up. Don't let your peers fool you into thinking that you can coast through your senior year. College recruiters look at your grades for this year, especially for your first semester. Then there's the SAT. Hopefully, you've taken it a couple of times during your junior year, but in the fall of senior year you need to take it once more.

The biggest part, though, is the application process itself. Each college requires a long, time-consuming application, and you need to apply to more than one. I make sure my students apply to at least three. Some of them, who feel certain that they're going to go to one college or another, ask me why. Well, maybe you've got your heart set on one particular college, but what if you just don't make the cut that year? Always make sure you apply to a couple of "safe" schools, where you know you have a good chance of getting in, in addition to your dream school.

When you're filling out the application, follow the directions. You can hand-write quite a bit of the information, but only do that if you've got nice penmanship. If the admissions officers can't read your application, that's not going to be helpful for you: use a typewriter instead. Your local library should have one you can use.

Different college applications require different things, but all of them request your financial information, letters of recommendation, and essays. I talk about financial aid below. As for the letters of recommendation, get as many as you can. I like to see students request letters from their community service advisor and minister as well as from their teachers. When they hear from people who have known the student in different capacities, I think it gives admissions officers a more complete picture of the student's personality and abilities.

Only ask for letters of recommendation from people who know you well. This is when the hard work that you've put into building relationships at your school comes in. If you haven't gotten to know any of your teachers as well as you may have liked, ask them for an honest answer when you ask them to write you a letter of recommendation. Most of them will tell you whether or not they feel comfortable writing one. You may have to hunt a little, but it's worth it. You don't want a recommendation letter from someone who barely knows you—they won't have anything special to say.

As for the essay, that's your best opportunity to show the admissions officers who *you* are. It's very important. I've talked to many admissions officers and they all say that they place a heavy weight on the essay portion of the application. So take it seriously. It's not the time to be modest—tell them what you've done and who you are, and answer the questions with confidence. Then make sure you have a tutor or a teacher look over your essay when you're done with it, to check for grammar and spelling.

Finally, *mail everything in on time!* Don't let all your hard work go to waste because you weren't able to get yourself together for the deadline. Remind the people who are writing your recommendation letters when they need to be done; I have one student who puts a Post-It note with the deadline on each recommendation form she gives to her sponsors. Collect everything, put it in an envelope, and take it down to the post office yourself. You don't want to do any guesswork with the postage, and besides, you want to make sure that they put the appropriate postmark on your application.

Resources for Tip 8

- *The Fiske Guide for Getting into the Right College.* Edward B. Fiske and Bruce G. Hammond. Naperville, Ill.: Sourcebooks Trade, 2002.

9. Complete a comprehensive financial aid assessment for every college you apply to, but don't depend on the school's financial aid alone. Look into private grants and scholarships.

If you're poor, you're going to have *two* part-time jobs during your senior year: applying to college and applying for scholarships. Don't depend on the colleges to give you all the money you need to go to college. Very few of their financial aid offices are that generous.

Even if you manage to get a full scholarship, it won't cover everything. It may cover your tuition, for example, but what about your room and board? And college comes with all kinds of hidden expenses that you won't know about until you get there: school fees, books, new clothes, a computer. These hidden expenses can cost thousands of dollars.

The answer is private scholarships. There are lots of them out there, and many of them go unclaimed year after year because no one applies for them. The key is knowing where to look, and giving yourself lots of time for a long, exhausting process.

Start looking as early as the tenth grade. Not all college scholarships are offered to seniors—quite a few of them are offered to high school students as young as fifteen years old. The best way to find out about national scholarships is to look through books that list them—you can find them at your library, or buy one at the bookstore. It'll be a worthwhile investment. The Internet is another great source of information, and often you can get free access at your local library.

You should also ask around your community about local scholarships. Even small towns have local organizations that offer scholarships to promising students, and the only way to find out about these is to ask. Some of the most likely sources include local branches of national membership organizations, like the Rotary Club and the NAACP.

The same rules apply to these applications as to your college ones. Follow the directions. Be neat and professional. Don't downplay your achievements, but don't embellish them, either! If you need letters of recommendation, ask the same people who are writing your college application letters. It's no big deal for them to print out another copy of the same letter.

Some scholarships require an interview, and I advise students to take it as seriously as they would a job interview or a college interview. That means wearing professional clothes, even a suit, to the interview. Practice possible questions with a friend before you go to the interview. Some of the ones my students hear over and over again are: "What does education mean to you?" and "What are your plans for the future?"

Resources for Tip 9

I laugh at the titles, but the *For Dummies* series has done some great work on this subject:

- *Free $ for College for Dummies.* David Rosen and Caryn Mladen. Indianapolis: For Dummies Publishing, 2003.

- *College Financial Aid for Dummies.* Herm Davis and Joyce Lain Kennedy. New York: Hungry Minds, Inc., 1997.

- The College Board has a great website with lots of scholarship listings. They sell a book, too, but the Internet is free. Have a look at www.collegeboard.com.

- For your interviews, look for affordable professional clothing at a local charity store, like Goodwill or the Salvation Army. You might want to ask a trusted adult to accompany you to the store for advice on what to pick.

- There is a website for finding the best prices on college textbooks: www.directtextbook.com.

10. You've been accepted into college. Congratulations! But remember that college is a whole new game. In many ways, your hard work has just begun.

Once you've made it in, get ready for the challenge that is college. If you're a student, and you've managed to get through the college application process all by yourself, you'll be a step ahead of your peers, because you have discipline and motivation. But very few students get through the process alone, and even those who do are surprised at what awaits them in college.

You have to be a self-starter in college. No one is going to care if you skip your classes, fail your tests, or don't eat for a week. There won't be anyone to check on you—not your parents, not your high school mentors, and certainly not your professors. You will be expected to be an adult, and you'll have to take care of yourself like one.

You can learn some of those skills ahead of time by learning how to cook, balance a checkbook, and set an alarm clock. If you can, talk to students who are already in college before you go. Find out from them what they wish they'd known before they went to college. If you don't know any college students, ask your favorite teacher or a wise person in your community for advice.

College will also be a challenge for you academically. If you went to a public school in a poor neighborhood, you'll find yourself behind some of your peers. *This isn't a reflection on your intelligence or your ability.* It's a reflection of the hand you were dealt—but don't complain about it or use it as an excuse to fail. All colleges have tutoring programs. Get extra help if you need it. And be prepared to sacrifice a little more. Sometimes when your new friends in college are going out for the evening, you may need to stay inside and study. But just remember what you went through to get here, and that sacrifice won't seem like a great one.

Resources for Tip 10

- *College Survival.* Greg Gottesman, Daniel Baer, and friends. 6th Edition. New York: MacMillan Press, 2002.

- *The Ultimate College Survival Guide.* Janet Farrar Worthington and Ronald Farrar. 4th edition. Lawrenceville, N.J.: Peterson's, 1998.

- *How to Study: Suggestions for High-School and College Students.* Arthur W. Kornhauser. 3rd Edition. Chicago: University of Chicago Press, 1993.

Good luck!

Acknowledgments

Oral Lee Brown

The Promise was a step back in time for me. I stepped back not just to 1987, when I adopted my original class of students at Brookfield Elementary School, but all the way back to the 1950s when my life experiences began to shape and mold me into the person I am today.

The first two women I have to thank are the ones who have been with me since those early years. One of them is my mother, Nezzie Bivins, to whom I offer all my success. The second is my elementary school teacher, Miss Grace. She was the first person who told me, "Oral Lee, you can be what you want to be." I have not seen her since 1957, but I think about her every day of my life.

There were many other people who made the road I have had to travel a little more accessible, and I have nothing but the highest gratitude for their unconditional love. To first name some of my siblings: my brothers EQ and CQ Bivins, and my sister Willie Walls and her husband Paul Walls, who raised me from the time I was twelve years old until I turned eighteen. To the four of them I want to say thank you and I will never forget what you did for me.

To my daughters, Lynn Channel and Phyllis Darrell, I love

Acknowledgments

you. To my three grandsons, Amonya, Lamonte Jr., and Emeka, keep up your schooling. To my four granddaughters, Tomora Marie, Michelle Roschell, Sharquetta, and Byresha, I want you to start preparing for the great years you will have ahead of you.

Mrs. Frances Holmes, Mrs. Beverly Clack, and my adopted mother, the late Mamie Hall—you are the greatest and I love you all.

To all my nieces, nephews, family, friends, and all of those who have supported the foundation over the years, I would like to thank you for your love and support. And last but certainly not least, I would like to thank the entire Osborne family. You have been a blessing from God.

Caille Millner

I could not have completed this without the constant love and support from my family: Joyce and Steven Millner and Jowcol Vina in particular. I also owe an enormous debt of gratitude to the people who have helped me get to where I am today—there are too many to thank, but certainly Sandy Close, Brandon Walston, Marcus Mabry, Tom Masland, Anthony Walton, Werner Sollors, Stanley Joseph, Amelie Von Briesen, Frank Scatoni, Greg Dinkin, and Ellis Cose belong on that list. Thank you to Janet Hill for seeing this project through to completion. Special thanks to Marcia Gordon for her research assistance.

⳩   262   ⳩

A final message from Oral Lee Brown:
All of my proceeds from this book will be donated to
the Oral Lee Brown Foundation.
To learn more about the Oral Lee Brown Foundation
please call us at (510) 430-3041, or
visit www.oralleebrownfoundation.com.

About the Author

Oral Lee Brown was selected as one of *Glamour* magazine's Women of the Year in 2002, and appeared on the *Today* show as part of its People Who Make a Difference series. She has also been a guest on *The Oprah Winfrey Show*, *NBC Nightly News with Tom Brokaw*, and *Courage*, hosted by Danny Glover. She has received numerous awards, including the California State Lottery Hero in Education Award; the Ten Most Influential People Award, given by San Francisco mayor Willie Brown; and the Madame C. J. Walker Award. She lives in Oakland, California.